COME GET THESE KIDS!

A Parent's Guide to Navigating the School System

"Come Get These Kids! is an engaging and necessary reframe for parents who find themselves having to balance work with the reality of present school system changes. It lays out clever insights creating opportunities to be more involved in our children's lives, even post Covid-19 pandemic."

Malcolm-Jamal Warner
Actor, Poet, Musician, Writer, Director

".... the book is a signature of Josiah's life quest to transform Comm-unity ...and that we may all sit at the table of Life's success ... a comprehensive education system for all is the door ...."

Bill Green
Former Director of Multicultural Engagement and Support (May 2020), Consultant Independent Contractor for Multicultural Development

"This book serves as a reminder that parents who struggle with the educational system are capable of advocating for their child."

De'Vonna Pittman
Author of My Pretty…and its Ugly Truth, a Memoir

COME GET THESE KIDS!

A Parent's Guide to Navigating the School System

DR. JOSIAH JACKSON

A Division of J Ltd LLC
7701 Golden Valley Road #270105
Minneapolis, MN 55427
www.josiahjackson.com

In this book, the stories and experiences are based on real events in the classroom. However, the names of some individuals and places are fictitious.

All scripture taken from the King James Version Bible

ISBN 978-1735472201

Cover design by J Ltd LLC

Send all correspondence to:

J Ltd LLC
c/o Josiah Jackson
7701 Golden Valley Road #270105
Minneapolis, MN 55427
www.josiahjackson.com

Acknowledgements

I thank God for giving me another opportunity to write. I wanted to write this book in June. God had other plans. Due to COVID-19, I started writing the book in May and finished by the end of June. All praise, glory, and honor to God.

I absolutely cannot go without mentioning the special people who were always there when I needed prayer, a think tank, or advice. I thank God for my family, friends, and colleagues who encouraged me to stay the course while completing this book. Kim Brooks, the exceptional book coach, thanks for keeping me focused while writing this book. Natalie Woods Leffall, thank you for editing the manuscript. Also, I thank all the parents that I worked with during the beginning months of COVID-19, who sought my expertise as a teacher and parent advocate to successfully navigate the school system and distance learning. Thank you!!

As we move forward during this intense time in America, know that you have made it this far. You are a winner!

This book is dedicated to all the parents I served and encouraged. Thank you!

Table of Contents

Introduction

The critical role I played as both teacher and parent advocate was to empower the well-being of parents. As a teacher, I have gained valuable lessons and insight from many of the parents and families I worked with over the years. I had always enjoyed working with family crises and did so with ease. Unlike most teachers, I grew to appreciate the hard work and dedication of many working parents whether they were single or married. The significant difference was many single household parents found themselves in need of more support due to their schedules and lack of knowledge of the school system. Knowing this, I would often hear, "Would you help me?" I was not one to advertise my expertise to school districts or even to the world, but somehow, young working women found me and needed guidance. Families that experienced hardships through finances, loss of homes, lack of funds to further education, children in need of parental supervision, or even mothers in need of relaxation, somehow gravitated towards me. It all boiled down to needing help from someone and somewhere. And, yes, we often need someone, whether a mentor, coach, or friend to help guide and nurture us throughout our lives.

Like many, I had a busy schedule that involved establishing a plan. In the beginning, teaching a class full of students felt scary, however, over time, it became easier. There was so much to grasp. From preparing lesson plans, learning classroom management, teaching student's relevant curriculum, to scheduling and communicating with parents and meeting with the community. I had to turn in reports for my daily schedule and management operation that required time to plan and write.

Woven into my teaching and advocacy moments were tough issues. Consequently, we all have our rocky days when everything is not going well. You must see this through the lens of a teacher.

There were countless experiences of parents making school choice decisions, seeking help for the right school staff to work with their child(ren), and signifying their need for help. That was the true benefit of working and helping families. From time to time, unexpected experiences proved that not all families could handle what they encountered through daily living. There were moments when some parents used excuses not to show up at school to meet the teacher regarding their children. It never stopped me from pushing them to the next level.

I stood in a position that gave me freedom to visit families in their homes. I took them to doctor, dental, and teacher conference appointments at school. For obvious reasons, developing working relationships with parents was vital. It was quite interesting to note that many families found themselves navigating the school system like a maze. Amazing! No really, a maze. They found themselves wandering around looking for answers. Sometimes the answers were in front of them, other times they were hard to find. It was all new to them. After years of teaching, it never occurred to me that some parents used my suggestions, and some did not.

I found myself tackling target issues that many parents continue to face right now during this worldwide Coronavirus Pandemic attack. A teacher's job seemed to never end.

Caring:

School buildings may have closed their doors, but my caring spirit remained open. One year, a few days before the last day of school, I started what I called, An Open Letter to My Students. It was an informal letter that spoke positive affirmations to each of my students. The goal was for them to share the letter with their parents and keep those words for the rest of their lives. Right now, I want to share something similar with you before moving forward in this book.

Dear Parent(s),

This is an exciting time in your life to take what you have and build on it. You may have gone through hard times and no one may have seemed to care, but you are here on purpose for a purpose. What you possess inside is the cornerstone for your child's future. You are like a huge beautiful tree. When your child looks up, they will see all your roots of pain, sorrow, love, and joy and desire to grow up like you. No matter the mistakes (they happen) every experience is a part of your growth. As you stand back and take look at who you are and who you desire your child to become, know that you are standing in the right place, at the right time to make new change happen. You are royalty!

Love, Ms. Jackson

The letter above is like what I gave each of my students. Like them, I treasure you too. I most enjoyed seeing your students learning about life. In writing this book, my heart's cry is that parents see what is happening in the school system or online, through distance learning, and become compelled to make necessary changes for all children.

The Set Up:

Recently, fires have erupted across America. From the President of the United States, to the COVID-19 Pandemic, social distancing concerns, racism, and politic agendas regarding state governors and mayors, fear and anxiety sweeps across our land. Naturally, I am go-getter. I am someone who likes to ignite and encourage with fire or put out fires with love and change. So, when I see the school system and parents standing between a rock and a hard place or in the valley of decision, it becomes a teachable moment.

Parental Support

Parents have rights! It was always a joy to see parents learning new strategies and then activating what they learned. You have potential. As parents, you know very well the tough days you encountered during school sessions. Regardless of where you stand now, your child's performance is always at the forefront. It is about what you want to see happening now. Does it matter how are you treated? Absolutely! In this hour, a new dilemma arrived and that is whether school buildings open or remain online through distance learning? Whichever decision is made, the tools provided in this book will guide you. A parent's job never ends.

Now imagine a windy, bright, sunny day. You are at home, working hard to finish a major project. Typically, you are alone while your children are away at school. You settle in with your cup of coffee or tea, sit at your computer, and before you can began typing, you hear, "Mom what do I do now?" The look on your face says, not now, while your body, mind, and soul, quickly, yells back, "Not now. I'm working!" Your precious little ones have now invaded your quiet workspace and now you all are stuck alone in the house. Before you know it, you are out of your chair and leaning over your child's iPad attempting to help them but finding it difficult to comprehend their work. In a quick second, you storm out of the room, run down the hall, shut the door behind you and scream, "COME GET THESE KIDS!"

This book evolved after hearing from many parents that I worked with and some I met for the first time. I share experiences as a teacher and advocate, while at the same time suggesting tips and ideas for working effectively with your children. During the pandemic, you may have lost hope and became overwhelmed with daily life tasks. You may decide that some strategies and suggestions work well while others simply do not work. This is a time to occupy that space and get involved.

Chapter One

Stuck in This House

What no school?! As a teacher, I longed for the day when school was out. There I was, waiting for Spring break which was in two weeks on March 23, 2020. Whew! I had been busy finishing a dissertation, working full-time as a substitute teacher at a middle school, ministering to others, taking rest breaks here and there, and somehow still finding the time to connect with family and friends. At the same time, I was planning my first vacation trip of the year in May. So, there I was, looking forward to my break, while working. Suddenly, there was a major change. An unexpected and sad change. It was the Coronavirus pandemic (COVID-19). Yes, that is what it was … a plague. A plague from the enemy! As Psalm 91:10 says, *there shall no evil befall thee, neither shall any plague come nigh thy dwelling* (KJV).

It all began on Friday the thirteenth. Based on the popular horror movie, many believe Friday the thirteenth is a day of terror. I am not superstitious, and you should not be either. Friday, March 13, 2020 was a good day. I received the best news!

I got up that morning doing my usual routine. I started the day with my personal prayer, participated in a 4:00 a.m. and 5:30 a.m. prayer conference call. Then, I listened to my favorite gospel radio station, while getting dressed for work. I checked my emails and had my usual phone call with my sister while packing my bags and lunch. I put my bags in the car, phone on the seat, started the car, and drove off.

I arrived at school only to notice one other car in the parking lot. Immediately, I had several thoughts, “Did I miss an email? Did I miss a meeting? What happened?” No one called me. I drove by the other car to talk to the person inside, hoping to find out what was going on. It was fellow staff member. He told me school was closed. The school sent an email, after I had left home, telling everyone to not show up. Well, no problem, I thought. I would just go the store, pick-up a few things and go home. That was the beginning of learning something big happened. Then again, it was the relief and release of being off for the next few months that excited me. Early Spring Break was in session. Yay!!

I drove to the grocery store for essential items, Kleenex, toilet paper, water, napkins, and cereal. My goal was to go in the store, get what I needed, and return home to relax. Sounds easy, right? Wrong!

While in the store, I walked to the toilet paper aisle and I was shocked. What was going on? The whole shelf was empty. Empty! Did I miss something? Did they have a sale? And if so, it must have been, a good sale because the whole shelf was empty. Not only was the toilet paper wiped out, but some of the other items were gone too. I could not focus! I left the store and went to another one. When I arrived at the next store, I was amazed! The shelves were empty at that store too. Okay something was going on and I had to know. Desperate for toilet paper, I went to a third store. I was finally able to get the items I needed there. Now I needed to get home and find out what was happening. I left the store and hurried home, after three hours of a wild goose chase for toilet paper.

I learned about the Coronavirus Pandemic (COVID-19). It is a disease that endangered the lives of many. Fortunately, some people survived it. By Sunday, news reporters announced that on Monday, March 15, 2020, all schools including colleges and universities would be closed. I was excited for an early break. Over the past three months, I had been cussed at, pushed, talked about, and ignored by students I had vowed to educate and love. I am sure some other teachers and staff were also relieved. After teaching in classrooms with troubled children, a break is always good. I was thrilled and ready for a break, to have peace, and quiet.

Suddenly, I started to think about parents who had no access to computers, educational resources, books, or other materials to keep their children engaged. I heard reports from the news and friends that many parents were outraged because school was closed, with no opening date scheduled. They were stuck at home with their children.

During a recent visit with a parent, we discussed juggling childcare, education and working from home. I was laid off, so honestly, I was thinking, "Yay, I have a break!" After listening to her, I said, "Even though, I have sympathy for you, now you get to see what I go through on a daily basis." I explained, "You will have to create a schedule for their learning, your work, cooking, and free time for everyone." We looked at each other and laughed. As I walked away, I laughed to myself and then I turned around and yelled, “Call me if you need me. After all, you will be home with them all day.”

A lot of parents really have no idea what we – teachers go through daily. Anyway, a break was needed for all of us – well, surely for me. However, because I am compassionate and concerned about families, I quickly started gathering materials and resources that I had in my house. Whether those materials were books, papers, or whatever a parent could use, I gave it to them. I specifically was looking for parents who absolutely had no resources. I made phone calls and found some of those parents. I started story time on Zoom. This worked. It was rewarding for me and fulfilling for parents. It provided a need for a few families while they and we all worked from home.

Even though, I enjoyed my job, I also knew what some parents and children were facing, especially in homes where there was no love and nurturing, I imagined home life for these kids was not too pretty, but I couldn't do much about it at that moment. Parents were stuck. Stuck does not mean you have to sit on a log and remain isolated. And being stuck does not mean it is the end of the world. When you feel stuck, you stop, and you think about where you are and how to move forward. You may be a parent feeling stuck right now. You may be thinking, "I'm stuck in this house with these children!" "What am I going to do?" "How could this happen?"

So, when the Coronavirus pandemic (COVID-19) happened and schools were closed the first week, I remember thinking, "Now parents can really see what we teachers go through at school." After learning the shut-down was going to be longer, I started hearing more news reports of parents complaining or comments like "When will school begin ?", "I have no idea what I am doing!", "How do I teach and do my work?", "I don't know what to do.", "Help me! I don't know what I am doing.", "When will summer school or camp begin?" Come get these kids!" A lot of questions, and few answers, but basically miserable for parents and some teachers. Since, I was a substitute teacher, I was laid off. Therefore, I did not have the experience of teaching distance learning. I had plenty of time to relax, write, and enjoy my days at home.

So here it was mid-March when the news of the Coronavirus pandemic (COVID-19) was announced. The first time we heard about it was when news reporters announced the outbreak of COVID-19, which showed up in the Western Pacific and European regions before widely spreading to the United States. COVID-19 began affecting lives all over this nation. Suddenly, the whole world turned upside down. It was one of those moments when time was asking you, "Are you going somewhere?" Or was time telling us, "Sit down. Take a break. You have all the time you need." Before I share some suggestions, I want to share a few examples and situations that I dealt with while teaching which signaled that I needed this gift of time for myself.

Have you ever been in a situation or place where you found yourself unable to move? You look up and you just cannot move. But, because you are such a perfectionist and always trying to prove to yourself that you can accomplish almost anything, you overlook the fact that maybe there is a reason for your inability to move. There you are … working hard, wiggling, and moving your way out. After several attempts, you settle in and realize no matter how smart you are or how much all that wisdom and knowledge is working for you, you are still stuck. Stuck in either the same place, a position that will not allow you to move. The frustration and stress begin to settle in, and you are now faced with anger because all the power in you failed. You now have remained in this environment baffled and unmovable. Thinking to yourself what next? How did I get here? How can I get out? Yes, that is what being stuck is all about. Your mind, body, and spirit are blocked and jammed for a moment.

Being stuck is like driving down a long dark road, and out of the blue, a deer runs across the street. To avoid hitting the deer, you swerve the car and slam on your breaks. That quick movement caused you to stop and remain stuck for a moment.

I remember before and even after I started teaching, I found myself stuck in a lot of situations. Many of these situations only allowed for me to be stuck for a moment. But each situation surely was not something I wanted to experience again. One of those situations happened while I was in college studying to be a teacher.

I was excited to start my teaching experience. Then, it was called, practicum. This was when you practiced your teaching skills in a classroom before graduating and getting hired to work in a classroom. Of course, the instructors always added that the practice was just that, practice. It was to allow me to activate some skills, but my experiences were going to be different once I was hired.

For my practicum experiences, I taught at three different schools, two elementary and a middle school. These schools gave me the experience of teaching with a teacher and their students. At least I did not have to grade papers and or attend meetings. The elementary schools were easy. I was able to interact with students. The teacher who mentored me was helpful, and I had a good experience.

When I went to the middle school, everything started out smooth until one day when the teacher did not show up for class. She was absent for the day. The teacher did not tell me she was going to be gone nor did she prepare me for any lessons for the students. I walked into the school believing it was going to be another smooth sailing day. I was going to follow the plans given to me.

Well that day, I had to think and act quickly. I had seven periods to get through and I was not sure what to teach. However, everything worked in my favor. The middle school classes I was training in were home economics – cooking classes. I absolutely loved cooking, so at least I was not nervous about any lab assignments. Since the teacher was gone, they sent a substitute to help in the classroom, since I was not licensed. The sub allowed me to do most of the teaching, even though I was still training.

Upon learning that I had to lead this and all the other six classes, I found myself stuck. I could not go back home, and I could not just give up and say, I cannot do this today. Well, I could have, but that is not what went through my mind. Up for the challenge? Yes. Then, I asked those questions, what do I do? Will I be able to manage all the students without their assigned teachers? That day, with the help from the substitute teacher assigned to the class, I was able – to manage the students and get through the day without any interruptions. As mentioned before, I immediately had to think of a good plan to not only get through the day, but to successfully make sure every student was on task. The first class was a little easy for me. I was able to give them an assignment and then instructed them to work on their lab projects. That day, each class was making pancakes. Whew! That was easy. No one made a huge fuss or mess with the assignment. I told the class to review their notes and then proceed to the lab assignment. I felt stuck for a moment, but I had help from others. I was nervous teaching and performing by myself, especially since I was not sure if my teaching skills were polished. But that day I did well. What seemed like being stuck then, was an opportunity to take the time to evaluate the situation, find a solution, and execute the plan.

You may not have experienced my exact teaching moment, but I know you have experienced moments when everything was going well, you were confident, feeling good, feeling better than good. You were on top of the world, nothing could knock you down or pop your bubble. You were on top of your game. You were moving and grooving. Even if something popped up, you knew exactly how to combat it and turn it around. Yes, you knew exactly what to do.

You were a planner. All your plans were in order. You were happy to get your children up, get them ready for school, cook breakfast, drive them to school, and wave goodbye as they entered the school building. You did not see them again until three or four that afternoon when they returned home.

While they were in school, you were either working from home or working at an office. There you were enjoying your job or pretending to enjoy your job. Drinking coffee and eating those office donuts all day. Life was good. You were not bothered because you knew in a few hours you and your child would return home, maybe talk a little, and eat dinner. That was your day, and nothing was going to change that until you were ready to make those schedule changes. Then suddenly, you hear that dramatic horror movie music and your world stops right before your eyes.

Do you know what it is like wondering what to do on a rainy and snowy day or when school is out? Of course, you do! You sit by the window, watch the weather, and wish you were somewhere else. Seriously, this was a different type of situation. What do you do when school is out, and you are at home with your children? It is like being stuck in the house. You feel stuck! What are you stuck in and why do you feel stuck? Sometimes when we are stuck, we do not know where to go or what to do. We think we must deal with the situation on our own. This is not one of the moments to say, "Whoa, is me!" Yes, you may feel or get stuck, but you can get up and move from this place. The one thing that I noticed as a teacher was that parents often called at a time when it was convenient and best for them. Whether they already had a final answer or not, they always wanted to get a teacher's thoughts and expert opinion.

School choice can be overwhelming. It takes time, time you sometimes do not have. This is good because in the next chapter, you will learn how to make a schedule and keep to it while being forced to stay at home with your children. Once you pass this phase of getting organizes, your life will be a lot easier. Once you accomplish the first phase, the next thing becomes easier and life gets better.

Parents have power! I am here to let parents know they can teach, advocate, and promote their child, and they can do it by themselves. I know it looks and sounds scary, but you can do it. What can you do? You can provide and make a way for your children? You can do it. I believe in you. Again, the power is in you to help educate and encourage your child. Parents do not give up on your children and yourself.

So, you say, “Stuck in this house.” Yes, you are stuck in that house - well for now and maybe for a while. I know many of you are thinking, “If I had a magic wand … poof … my children would be back on campus, in the classroom.” Well, brace yourself for the long haul. Let us get to it. While being stuck in the house, how can you make the best of it?

Let me help you by sharing some suggestions and tips you can use while you are stuck in the house with your children. These tips are not written in stone, so, feel free to come up with your own tips on what to do while stuck in the house with your children:

Tip #1: Organize, organize, and organize

Find time to organize your thoughts, your schedule, and your children’s schedule. When you brainstorm, you see the picture clearer. Decide what is important to you and your children. Again, being stuck in the house does not have to be boring or mundane. Yes, I know one or two days inside could be fine, but week after week or month after month, can be a long time to be confined. Find what makes you happy. Organize prayer or meditation time, game time, and/or comedy hour time. Relax, sleep, make art projects, do things together. Okay, so you are probably thinking, have you seen my child? Yes, I have seen every one of them! In my 28 years of teaching, I have experienced every type of child on the planet. Remember, you are the parent, the guardian, the take-over person for the day, the nanny, the Sherriff, the loving mom, the supportive dad. Perhaps you are the mom or dad too busy to figure this out. Believe me, I know you are busy. I have watched parents drop their children off at school and drive off like a NASCAR racer, trying to get to work! I was stuck with their children all day. Yes, just like you, I was stuck, but the world did not come to an end, so you can do this. I know you can!

Tip #2: Invest time with your child

How well do you really, really know your child? Let us start with the teenager. Does he
or she have habits, secrets that you do not know about? This is perfect, new bonding time. Ask your teen what they like to do. It could be hard getting the answers you want. However, you can suggest going to a movie, listening to music – checking out their music selections, having fun creating new dance moves, and playing games on the internet.

Tip #3: Establish better communication with your child at home

Communication is the key in every relationship. Take time to talk with one another. Just talk! Communicate! You talk, they listen. They talk, you listen. Simple enough, right? Sadly, many parents and children relationships are not like this. Parent-child communication in many homes is almost nonexistent. I am not a psychologist, but I do know the value of two-way communication in the home. You may have vested interest in other things but find the time to invest in and listen to your children.

Communicate with your children. Once school buildings open again, there will be several days students will have off. Practice communicating better with each other now. We are here at this moment, the big break. I know most of you are not too excited about this "big break." And, others are way too excited. Unfortunately, some cases and situations became serious. For example, dealing with physical, emotional, or mental abuse, death, or domestic violence. What do you do when you are stuck in the house and these situations are present? I encourage you to get out, find a safe place, and tell someone. I know this sounds like a quick answer. It is not. I understand the seriousness of abuse and do not want you or your children in an unsafe environment. If this is you, call local or national hotlines and get help.

Communication is the key when you feel stuck. For parents who feel stuck, take time for yourself, even while you feel trapped in the house. Having someone to walk alongside you always helps. Collaborate with others. Meanwhile, interact with your child by communicating statements that help redirect them.

Here is an example of an opening conversation:

Parent: How do you feel about attending school online – distance learning?

Child: I had a good day.

Parent: What did you do that made it a good day?

Child: We played my favorite toss the ball game during morning meeting.

Parent: Great, it sounds like you really enjoy playing the game.

At this point, as the parent, you can elaborate. You could give your child advice on how to continue enjoying classroom game time and remain positive throughout the day.

Tip #4: Create

Use your creativity and create new products and projects. Not everyone will be able to do this, but you could try. Try something new, a new craft or hobby. For example, make a personalized mask for your family.

Tip #5: Reach out to others

Find time to connect to other families. This is a great time to reach out to fellow parents who are in need or in the same place as you. You can share Ideas, resources, and learn how other families are coping with being at home during the pandemic.

Tip #6: Join a group

Join a new mom, parent, or family group. There are several online self-help or meet up groups you can join via the internet. You do not have to go anywhere. You can join online, share your experiences, and learn from others. Connecting with others online is helpful, especially when you are not able to physically interact due to social distancing. Be sure you visit websites that are safe, promote well-being and have strong cyber anti-bullying and child predator monitoring. For example, using Zoom or Google, or GoTo meeting sites that help you connect with families or organizations is safer than an online chat site. The good thing about online groups is that you can join from the comfort of your home and remain safe and productive.

Tip #7: Call others for help and support

Sometimes you need others to listen to you, especially when you have a great deal of concerns on your mind.

Tip #8: When visiting schools or talking with others, ask questions

Asking questions helps you understand what to look forward to when you enroll your child. Ask questions such as, do they teach culturally relevant curriculum, what is the ratio of teacher to students in the classroom and what is their policy on bullying?

Tip #9: Keep updated with current and school news

With the wake of the pandemic, systematic racism, distance learning, homeschool, and some schools reopening at the forefront, this is a good time to discuss current news with your child. Help them understand how to protect themselves from the Coronavirus – COVID-19 by wearing masks and gloves and keeping 6 feet away when they are outside their home. Discuss with them historical racial tensions in America to what they are experiencing now. And whether they are in school or homeschool, ensure your children that they can challenge themselves in both places when they try to learn. Ask your children an open-ended question, such as: what do they think about what is going on in America?

Tip #10: Be responsible for checking materials and remaining updated

Use some social media sites on the internet to get the latest information on what is going on in the world. In most schools, many young people enjoy using social media sites, sadly for some wrong reasons, but there are many good websites that educate youth. This is another good reason for remaining connected to what they are viewing on the internet.

Tip #11: Read

Yes, read! Read something that piques your interest. Read books and articles on subjects that matter to you and your family. Read for enjoyment and learning new words and topics of interests. Most children shy away from reading because it looks so hard. Words can be frightening for a child who has not had someone to read to them or listen to them read. Not only children, reading words you do not know or understand can be scary for anyone, at any age.

I recently heard about adults challenging themselves to learn up to five new words from the dictionary every day. I was impressed, so I decided to accept the challenge.

I continue to at least learn one or two words throughout my busy day or week.

Reading can be fun. All too often, I have heard excuses from individuals – parents and school age children have said reading is too hard or not interesting. They would say, "I just do not want to read." Sadly, I discovered that many of those who shared they did not like to read, could not read. Illiteracy is a massive problem for many adults in America. "Adults with the least amount of schooling live below basic prose accounting for the largest percentage (55% -71%) of adults living below the federal poverty line" (Baer, J., Kutner, M., and Sabatini, J).[1]

You would be surprised how many adults, and now children, cannot read but work their way through life. The inability to read is real in the lives of many! Now you and your child have time to work on learning new words and reading. Ultimately, help your child read and comprehend

---

[1] Baer, et al

what they are reading. Start by reading for enjoyment and learning new words and topics of interests.

Here are some fun tips on finding enjoyment while reading together with your young child and/or teenager:

Tip #1: Read food labels, containers, candy wrappers, and boxes used from cooking meals

Tip #2: Read while you are driving. Read all the words in print (billboards, traffic signs, names on buildings, restaurants, - anywhere you see print.

Tip #3: Read comic books and magazines

Tip #4: Read labels on electronics, gadgets, bikes, computers, tablets. For younger children, read words on toys.

Tip #5: Read captions on television, computer screens, apps, and cell phones

Tip #6: Read from Kindle and other digital devices

Tip #7: Make up a story and read it

Tip #8: Make grocery or other lists and read them

Tip #9: Make up a game that involves reading or saying words

Tip #10: Practice writing down words or making up new words, then reading them

Tip #11: If you do not know the words, sound out the letters, use phonetic spelling to sound out words.

Tip #12: Reread books for clarity and identifying new concepts

Again, these are suggestions for how to encourage reading when you are stuck in the house with your children. Reading is a way to communicate with others while learning new words, adventures, and skills. After reading, discuss what you read to get a better understanding about the article or story. Allowing the material to become meaningful to you and an adventure for your child.

Chapter Two

I Do Not Have Time

Have you ever been so busy that you did not know what to do? So busy that you do not have time to look for the right school, make better life decisions for you child, or even ensure your children are going the right direction? Times and seasons go by so fast. When you look up, the school year will be over, and it will be time to enroll your children into school again. Soon, they will be out of the house and on their own. Okay, I will not push that far, but you get what I mean. When you are having fun, life moves quickly. Sometimes, you wonder how you ended up where you are in life. I have been there. Looking back, I am amazed how far I have come as a teacher and advocate.

School is out! To a parent and teacher, those are lovely words to hear, no matter what time of the school year the break comes. These are good words for some parents because they are ready to ship their children off to camp or to a relative's home. Again, looking back as a child, I remember hearing, "School is out" and thinking, "Oh no!" Those words meant my mom would have Bible study and prayer every day from 8:00 a.m. in the morning until noon in our house. For many parents today, school being out means it is time to ship their children somewhere else. As a teacher in the classroom, school being out signifies a break for me.

I was grateful for teaching in the classroom for five years, but then I had to take care of a terminally ill parent. That led me to taking a leave of absence from teaching. Though my teaching years were exciting, moving on to becoming a parent advocate was exciting too.

It was 2005 and schools had drastically changed – in my opinion – for the worse. I had not taught in the classroom since 1999 and had no desire to return to teaching. Many of my colleagues were taking early retirement or just leaving education due to the rise of extremely poor student and parent behaviors. I mean, who did these parents think they were? Some of these parents were rude and disrespectful. What I did know is that these parents needed help. Even though I found some parents to be problematic, I had a mission to fulfil. All jokes and personal concerns set aside; I was still commissioned to be a teacher. I had begun fulfilling my purpose and I needed to continue doing what God called me to do, teach families in and out of the class. I set out to do just that!

During that same year, I received an opportunity to become a parent advocate after answering an ad in the newspaper. I was excited because the description was what I call a "shoe in" job. Every skill and responsibility fit me perfectly. As some would say, "if the shoe fits, wear it." Well, I planned on taking those high heel shoes and wearing them. As I hoped, the shoe fit! I applied for the parent advocate position and was quickly hired due to my teaching credentials. From my first day as a parent advocate until the day we shut down, I ran. I put on my tennis shoes, I mean my high heel pumps and worked diligently on behalf of families who needed my assistance.

Day one arrived and my first assignment was to call parents to confirm whether they enrolled into school or still needed to enroll. I was to double check their school enrollment status. There was a list of about 20 to 40 families that I had to contact. I was excited because I had been away from teaching for 12 years. I was not ready to go back into the classroom, but I was ready to continue working with families. I never stopped doing that. I made it through day one of my new role as a parent advocate.

What I loved about this position was being able to do exactly what I wanted! Wow! I had never had a job where I could literally do what I wanted. The opportunities were endless. It was a like starting my own business. New position, new journey, and new families to help encourage and motivate. There is always a lesson in embracing a new assignment. I encourage you to take the new assignment, learn the lesson and move forward with joy.

My main role as a parent advocate was helping families understand the school system. I would accompany families to school conferences to meet about suspensions and special education - Individual Education Plans (IEP). I absolutely enjoyed this assignment because it allowed to two things: 1). I was able to use my experience in the classroom and sit on the other side and advocate for families. It was important that families knew what was truly was going on in schools. 2). I was blessed to meet new families. This was always a joy because it was an opportunity to encourage parents. Though, I enjoyed working with all families, some were difficult. Every family had their own dynamic situations.

Even though much of my assignment was to attend meetings with parents, sometimes sitting in those meetings made me feel stuck. I mean, the meetings were informative, but often boring. Yes, I said it, boring. By that I mean, meetings about the school's policies, not necessarily how to resolve the issue with the parents. Once the meeting was over and I received the information I needed, I was ready to work. Which leads me back to what is going on today.

It has been a few months now that schools have been closed and you are probably sitting there thinking, "Time? Who has time?" If you are reading this book, you have time. I know this sounds like a cliché, but time is on your side. Right now, you may be that parent feeling pressured, hopeless, tired, frustrated, agitated, bored, and simply at the end of either stuck in the house or stuck in life. School session is right around the corner. You may be searching for the best school, desiring to advocate for your child. Or you may be thinking, "It does not matter what school I send my child to, as long as it is just a school. As long as my child is placed in a school where they are learning." Wrong? Sorry, to burst your bubble, but this is not how you should be thinking about your child's education. Do not cut yourself and your child's education short. Your little one may be under or over five feet, but do not let sell yourself short. Do not allow searching for the right school and getting the best education for your child trip you up. After all, this is your pride and bundle of joy. That lawyer, doctor, millionaire, preacher, airline pilot, businesswoman or man, king, queen or even the future president of the United States! Yes, your child ... your precious little one has the potential to do great things. Get up, gather your thoughts and fight for their future. You can do it!

These few examples could help you. Next, I want to share a few examples of how you can make time for your precious little one, two, or ten. Making time for yourself and your kids will require sitting down (yes, you will have to sit down for this one). You can stand if you want, but you will have to find some time to work through a plan. You probably have not realized it, but you already have a morning routine. You do not think of it this way, but most likely you do the same thing every morning. Even if you switch up a little, you have scheduled time to accomplish your morning tasks. For example, you probably get up at the same time or close to the same, exercise, watch the morning news, yell at your children for waking you up too early, cook breakfast – or maybe you set out cereal? Your life is too busy to cook that good hot meal! That is okay, I feel you. Cold cereal is my quick fix too. My point is here is to prove you have taken time to establish routines. Start with the areas you have already mastered.

One year, a student was assigned to case load in late April. Yes, late in April, with less than 40 days of school left. I was told the student had a huge Individual Learning Plan. His I.L.P. was a 20 to50 page book. Yes, you heard me right, 20 to 50 pages long. Wow! That was how much was written about this child. Much prayer was needed for this situation. Prayer has always been my way of seeking God for everything. I remember sitting in a meeting going over all the notes for this new child that was scheduled to come to my class. The I.L.P. suggested this young East African American boy was troublesome. He had extreme behaviors that were out of control. It was written that he fought other children and sometimes the teacher. His history of negative behavior was also confirmed by one of the persons on his team. As I listened, I thought, "Now, I really need to meet this young boy." I prayed and asked God what was going on with this child. I skimmed through this thick 50-pages booklet. I was not interested in what others said. I wanted to see for myself. I wanted to meet the boy and his parents. So, the day came when I met the family. The young boy seemed like he was okay, but that did not say much for what I heard. Good thing I did not accept everything I heard. I could be very stubborn when it came to things I do not agree with. That was a good thing. Before showing up in my class, the "old" case worker told me that the student gets mad easily and fights quickly.

The day came when he entered my classroom. I observed him. I kept one eye on his behavior and kept an open mind. I watched, listened, and observed. I saw and heard nothing! All day I watched, I watched, and I watched, and I watched. This young boy did absolutely nothing. He helped me and was very polite. We got through day one without incident, but I thought surely, I would see something in the next few days. Well, the whole week went by and nothing, absolutely nothing. The student everyone warned me about gave me no trouble at all.

Once I learned this young boy was not anything like what was written about him, I informed my principal and those on the I.L.P. team. I also shared with his mom. She was ecstatic. She was happy that someone saw something different and cared about her son. Exactly! I felt the same way. When the student's mother heard my good news, she knew she had made the right decision. She was so happy that she took her son from his previous school. The boy's mom felt his old school had set him up for failure. She refused to let that happen. He made it through the end of the school year without any fights! He did not hit me or any of the other kids. He was fine and he passed the class. Everything that was written about him was either a lie or someone needed to write a really, long impressive report and make themselves look good. I really do not know. What I knew was, that report communicated the wrong information about this young man. I also felt if the child had exhibited any of the behaviors in his report, it was because someone or something bothered him. Was he operating out of self-defense or was it a cry for help? What impressed me most was his mother was willing to invest the time to ensure her child was treated fairly. She was not going to let her child get sucked into or through a system because of those trusted to care for him did not believe in him.

I did not expect it, but on the last day of school, my student's mother brought me a bag. Inside the bag was a thank you gift. She was so appreciative of what I had done as his teacher. She expressed her gratitude for how I saw and helped her son. She bought me a gift. It was not just a card and candy. She took the time to get me something special. That gift was a brand-new suit and perfume.

Then there was time when I worked with fathers, mostly single fathers raising their children. Brad did a wonderful job helping Selina who at the time was 7 years old. She was diagnosed with Alcohol Fetal Syndrome which resulted in her needing special education services. She did not do well at her first school, so Brad took Salina from that school and enrolled her into another. Unfortunately, the new school did not work out either. Feeling like he had no choice, Brad enrolled Selina back into the first school.

After going back and forth, Brad found our parent advocacy office and sought help on what to do. He was a loving father, struggling to understand the school system and his daughter's symptoms. Selina was an impressive, busy young girl. She struggled with reading and comprehension in school, but her father was on top of his game. Brad made sure that despite his Selina's deficiencies, she would make it through school and succeed. Brad and Selina stayed with our program until we abruptly shut down. Five or seven years went by and I ran into Selina again. Currently, she was a junior in high school. I was delighted to know she maintained help from other social services. Selina was doing well in school. I was happy to learn that Brad was also doing well.

Success comes in all shapes, sizes, and forms. No one can dictate what it looks like for you or your children. Over the years, it has always been good to see parents and students I helped continue to receive the help they so desperately needed. Even if some families fell off, I am still happy to know that I was a part of their lives.

Some parents need help and others do not. This applies to young and seasoned parents. My role is to help in any way I can. After all, there is help there for whatever need you have within your life. There are many programs on television, radio, or in the community that help you become a better parent. I learned from many families and I helped them learn how to advocate on their own. It may seem scary, but you can do it. Whatever barriers you face, tackle them head on.

Some parents are struggling right now to make ends meet. They are trying to manage daily tasks, helping children with schoolwork, and working their jobs. Parents do not have time, energy, enough strength, knowledge, education, know how. They lack an understanding of how the school system works and how to fight for their child.

So out of frustration, many parents are saying in either a loud or quiet way, “Come get these kids!”

I hear you, loud and clear! It is not necessarily the parents who are illiterate or intimidated by education jargon that yells, “Come get these kids.” This cry also comes from parents who are CEO’s, doctors, nurses, businesswomen and men, and entrepreneurs. Some parents are so busy juggling their job, making ends meet, and now taking more time to watch their child during the six hours that they used to be away at school, but are home now due to COVID-19. For this reason, school became a haven and place of relief for students and parents. It is not that some parents do not have time. Some have time, but do not know what to do with that time. I understand these mothers and fathers. But to say, “I’m stuck” and do nothing about it, means you are giving up. It is time to develop a plan and get a schedule!

Speaking of scheduling, there was a time while

working as a parent advocate that we hosted parent's night. This was a night when parents would come together and discuss concerns about schools and/or parenting. They could share ideas, thoughts, and get valuable parent resources. However, parents had to schedule the time to attend this event to get the material.

Scheduling and/or Planning:

Are you a person who likes to follow schedules or do you prefer to make your schedule as you go along? For example, when you get up in the morning, do you mentally plan or write down your goals for the day? Or do you just get up and keep moving until you fall out at the end of the night? Many parents think making a schedule helps them organize and get through the day. Then you have the parents who absolutely do not use a schedule, a planner, or write down goals. Do whatever works for you and your children. In my experience, I have found that making a schedule helps tremendously.

If you want to get something accomplished, scheduling and writing down goals helps you achieve and move further throughout your day, week, month, year, and life. It is like running a race. When you sign up, you know there is a finish line. You know where the finish line ends, and you head for it!

Developing a schedule or plan indicates you are looking towards to a brighter future for you and your child. Of course, life happens, so leave room in your plan for when things get off course.

A schedule is a guide, like this book. If you have never developed a plan – a real plan, the next few pages will help you get started. Typically, we do not think about making schedules or planning until we start on a project or want to get something done. As a parent, planning your days while juggling with other tasks can be hard. Where do you start?

Making schedules are important because they allow

you to set things in order. A planned scheduled brings organization to our life, your children's lives, school, home, and your family activities and lifestyle. The key is to make clear goals for how to live and maneuver it through life. You may be a new parent or experienced parent, but you can create and stick to a schedule!

Scheduling can be tedious. I mean, who likes to write out a schedule on a piece paper? Me! But I realize not everyone is like me. The funny thing is scheduling is something we do all day and every day. Whether we write it down, say it, or store it somewhere in our brain, our lives are run by schedules. It may not be an unorganized schedule, but it is a schedule.

Perhaps you are saying, "I don't' have time to create a schedule." I know, I know. We all have said or thought this same thing. However, when you think about it, you have a daily schedule or routine you follow every day. Try this quick exercise.

Think about today. Consider these questions and write down your answers:

What time did you get up?

What did you eat for breakfast?

What time did you get dressed?

When did you talk to your children and family members?

When did you exercise?

When did you watch the news?

Now, review your answers. Did you notice a routine? Were there some activities you routinely do every day? If so, this is your schedule. Whether you see it this way or not, you have a schedule – a daily schedule. Now, let us explore how to put your schedule together.

Putting a schedule together can be difficult. Establishing the right schedule for you and the children in your household is key to your success. It works! Prayer works! I encourage you to pray about how you choose to organize your life! Ask God to guide you in making the best schedule for your family. Do not get stuck here. God listens and He will get you through it.

What if school buildings do not open and children do not return to school for an extended period? What are you plans? Start scheduling now. If you are stuck now, you do not want to still be stuck when school starts. You must have a plan to educate and support your children if campuses do not open and children do not return. Begin with plan A, but it is perfectly fine to have a plan B, and maybe even C.

Here, I have the honor again to share some tips.

Tip #1: Develop a map, schedule, or plan with time and dates for yourself and the school year.

I mentioned this so many times above that you should have at least half page already. But if not, after reading this page, jot down some plans and make a schedule. This is particularly important. Have a regular schedule for your daily tasks. Plan, plan, plan, then practice, practice, practice. Put the plan in motion. Make it simple. You do not have to have an elaborate plan but have a simple one that works for you and your family.

As parents, you can have a lot on your "plate" and mind. I highly recommend making a personal schedule for yourself.

. Use the template located at the end of this book to start building your personal schedule. Just remember, your schedule should not just include dropping off your children at school and making a run for it! Make time for things you enjoy like going shopping, visiting the salon, getting your nails done, or spending time with friends. Self-care is essential. You must take care of yourself. After all, you are the parent, your child's first teacher, and the one they look up too for future success.

Tip #2: Help your child with their life goals.

I mainly am referring to school-age children and teens between the ages of 6 and 19. Write down what you want their future to look like. If they are old enough to understand this exercise, have your children help you with this exercise by sharing their dreams and goals.

Here is an example of a school day schedule that you can use:

6:00 a.m. – Get up for devotion, breakfast, or your time alone

6:30 a.m. – Make breakfast for your family

7:00 a.m. – Make sure kids are dressed and ready for school

7:45 a.m.- Drive children to school

8:00 a.m. – Drive to your office or back home to start your workday

3:00 or 3:30 p.m. – Pick-up kids from school and drive home

4:00 or 4:30 p.m. – Arrive home, eating a snack, gathering schoolwork, check emails

5:00 or 6:00 p.m. - Dinner time with my family

5:30 – 6:30 p.m. - Clean up the kitchen, decide on family or independent time, reading, take a walk, talk on the phone, or work on a project

7:00 p.m. – Family or relaxation time

8:00 p.m. – Checking with each other to see how your day went, preparing for the next day

9:00 p.m. – Put your children to bed

The above schedule is for weekdays. You can create a schedule for the weekend. When you have a schedule, do your best to follow it as much as possible. I write goals for myself every day. When you start each day with a goal, you feel better at the end of the day, knowing you accomplished something, even if it was just one goal. I am surprised at how many goals I get accomplished. What I do not complete, I simply add to the next day or week. Tracking your goals is a way to stay on track and accomplish what you need for that day, week, month, and year. We will talk about goals in another chapter. I also pray before making my list. I want to make sure God is in it. Only God knows what He planned for me to accomplish in a day. This is what scheduling is all about. You develop a plan, stick to it, and the rest is history.

Along with scheduling, it is important you look at what you did in the past and improve for your future.

Even if it seemed hard and long, having a schedule helps keeps you on track. You may already be a wiz at writing schedules and goals, at least you learned more about it, about yourself, and how to move forward with them. In addition to being stuck in the house, you have learned a few things to improve on where you are and where you child can be.

There are several other areas where making a schedule will be helpful:

Making schedules for important meetings and doctor's appointments

Making schedules for workshop dates and times

Making schedules for your child's tutoring, musical, acting or dancing sessions

Making schedules for programs and events, church, and outings

Making schedules for parent meetings and visiting other parents

Making schedules for play time at the park or on the town

Making schedules to visit and help others

Along with scheduling it is important to keep lines of communication open. Communication is the glue that holds the system together when ensuring all is well with you and your children.

Communicating with the school:

Though we communicate in three ways: visual (seeing), auditory (hearing), and kinesthetic (movement), understanding what works best for you and your child helps you better communicate. By understanding your child's school and educational language, you can determine whether the school is best for your child.

Communication is the key when it comes to expressing your needs and wants to others. It is the key to any working relationship. In this case, a working relationship with you, the parent, your child, and school or community is essential. The families I worked with were afraid to communicate because they were not sure if they were asking the right questions, communicating correctly, using the right words, or clearly stating their needs. Sometimes, they felt intimidated by the teachers or principal's language and attitude. Many parents were uneducated and did not feel the teacher or principal understood them. This is one reason many parents sent their children to school and left the school to do the rest.

Some parents felt like they could not help their children, so why bother. Some felt they would get talked about if they helped and surely talked about if they did not help. There was a strange communication gap and misunderstanding. It was a mess. These same parents felt the teachers and schools were the expert on their child's learning. Sadly, this was where many parents fall short. Ah, but today is your day! It is a new day. Here is where you, the parent, you can help. You can jump in and be a part of your child's education, even if you do not know what you are doing or how to do it yet. Remember, it is you and your child we are discussing here. This is your time to soar, to get it right and propel.

As I mentioned above, the families I worked with were genuinely concerned about ensuring their children had a voice at school. The fear of not having enough knowledge or experiences to advocate for their child was a major concern. Moms and dads were also concerned about the barriers that they faced while being in certain school districts. I was instrumental in helping them successfully learn how to advocate for themselves, while closing the communication gap between other parents, students, and staff. Parents were now able to obtain life skills and resources to help them with their children.

At the time, I utilized the parent sessions to help them better connect with schools and other families dealing with similar concerns. The biggest concern was that some of the parents had a lack of knowledge about student enrollment in various programs. Even though parents could enroll in a school of their choice, they would arrive at the school and suddenly realize it was not what they wanted.

Some schools advertised one thing and when families showed up to enroll, they found out the school had classes their children had not been exposed too. These were courses with material and knowledge unknown to their children.

As a parent, you always need important information

during the summer and anytime throughout the school year. Call the school before your child starts and get information on policies and expectations, the curriculum, and professional development plans for staff. By keeping the lines of communication open and staying on top of things, you are making sure your children remain on top.

Remember, I mentioned establishing communication with your child in chapter one. Go back if you forgot what I shared. Not only do you want to communicate with your child, but you still want to keep the lines of communication open with your child's school, as well. Open like a book.

Communicating with your child's school is especially important because sometimes teachers, principals, and school staff are so busy they forget and leave out information, sometimes important information that helps you succeed.

Here are some ways to keep the lines of communication

open with your child's school, even while you are working:

Tip #1: Learn about the school surroundings (in/outside the building)

Do not assume just because the school sends home announcements or flyers about something that they know what you are thinking. Most of these flyers and announcements are reminders to ensure you received them. It is up to you to inquire about what is happening and make sure you fully understand what is being sent home. By the way, with advanced technology, flyers come through email, on the school website, or via text message. Check all sources for information. Gone are the days of just word of mouth communication. Always check-in with the school on what is being sent home. Ask them for more details. You would be surprised how many times I worked with parents and schools, and they both were on two different pages. Do not assume anything. Find time to make those calls, send those emails, and double check on what is being communicated. Do not wait until something happens. You can pray until something happens, but do not wait until something happens. Work on being proactive.

Here is another good example of miscommunication. In the past, many parents I worked with really had no idea what type of school they wanted for their children. Some of these parents heard of a school but had no clue what that school offered. Choosing a school was like shopping for a new car, but not knowing what features you want to have. To learn about a school means, you should visit the school unannounced and announced. Make it a point to learn about the principal and staff. Ask and answering questions, such as: Is this the best school for my child? Is this the best atmosphere for my child? What type of children attend this school? Will staff go the extra mile to help my child get the best education? Does the staff genuinely like me and my child? Believe me, when you ask these questions to yourself and to school officials, you will discover if it is the right place for your child. Misunderstanding occur when parents do not do their research or talk to someone knowledgeable before enrolling their child into school.

Tip #2: Participate

Parental involvement is huge in schools. Parents can participate in PTO meetings, school board meetings, school events, and parent -teacher conferences. Many communities, schools, and businesses recognize the need for family partnerships. Every group or organization is not supporting you or your child's beliefs.

Tip 3: Listen

Listening to your child is golden. Keeping your eyes and ears open gives your access to what they need. When you do not know what or how to do, ask. Only you can improve your child's learning. Watch and listen to your child. They are watching and taking note of you. When you are involved with their learning, they appreciate you.

By creating an anxiety free environment, pay attention and follow through with your child's needs. Transition is hard for many students. Ultimately, listen to them, they are willing to change if you are aware of their needs. Listen to your child and expect the best from them at school and while distance learning.

Expect the Best:

Expecting the best. What does this mean? Expecting the best means making sure you understand everything you read, sign, and comprehend. If you do not know, then ask and get help.

As a parent, it is crucial to know what to do and how to help your child, especially in special education. There are many programs that offer free support. You are never alone with your child in any school whether it is public, private, charter, or homeschooled. I came across many parents who were overwhelmed. Many felt schools did not like them or their child. Therefore, I enjoyed advocating and showing parents how to advocate for themselves. This is very dear to my heart. I do not like families getting messed over just because they did not know or understand the rules or assignments.

I remember when I received a referral to help a young man in junior high school. He was on an Individual Learning Plan (I.L.P.). This young man was suspended. The adult taking care of him was his grandparent. This young man brought a knife to school and showed it to a few students. Once the school learned about it, they immediately suspended him. Briefly, during the meeting with the school, the grandparent learned that the principal planned on sending her grandson to another school.

I have taught in several different school districts in and out Minnesota. I learned that each district handles these situations differently. Anyway, the decision was for her grandson to be transferred to another school until the end of the school year. Technically, he was suspended or expelled for 45 days which meant he could not enter school again until mid-September of the following school year.

However, since I advocated for the student, the school was willing to work with the family. They reduced his suspension from 45 days to just a few days. If he did well, then he could stay at school for the rest of the year. The grandparent was pleased with this decision. She was not clear on how this was working for her benefit, but I encouraged her to place her grandson on a plan so he could remain at his school and not get transferred.

In the end, he was not transferred. This is just one of those examples of the power of communicating with the school, but also where the grandparent had no clue of what to do or understanding of what she was being told.

Some parents feel they must go along with whatever the school says. That is not the case. Again, since most parents feel they are not educated enough to help their children, they depend on the school system to do it for them. This is a good reason why you, as the parent, must show up and be present. Be visible from the beginning.

I do not like it when school's bully parents. But I do not like when parents get off easy either. Talk about students bullying each other, some schools do this with parents, especially if parents have no idea of what is going on.

Some parents really do want to be in the know and want to know how to support their child. As a parent, you have a right to say whatever you need to help your child succeed. What happens when parents are not active? What happens to those children? Some parents are not able help, but they can do their best.

Expecting the best is doing what you can with what you have … your voice. Whether you say something right or wrong, start with your voice. Make noise with your ideas and suggestions. This is how change begins.

Schools are always creating new programs. As

matter of fact, you can be a part of starting a new program. More ideas about this will be shared later. Sometimes these programs are designed to help students while at school and other times to keep students from enrolling or participating at school. In other words, some programs were designed without you in mind.

The good news was, once parents found there was someone advocating for them and helping them at school, they were excited. It made a big difference when parents were able to have someone knowledgeable walk side by side with them. Schools often use foreign language – language parents do not understand or comprehend. I do not think they mean to do. Like many industries, education has its own language. Just like you are learning to do better, schools must do better too. Who knows? After COVID-19, schools just might do better? Still, you matter … and your child matters.

As you expect the best, keep in mind that not

everyone expects you to be the best. You must prove to yourself and to your child that you are the best.

Setting Expectations:

As a matter of fact, students who consistently disrupt class and have extreme behaviors sometimes want attention. They feel that the more negative behavior they have, the more attention they will get. Interestingly, sometimes this looks like it works. It makes the teacher and other students in the classroom stop and pay attention. Sometimes, children who watch negative behavior feel it is an open door for them to behave the same way. After all, it looks like those exhibiting negative behavior seem to win everyone's heart. Once behaviors arise, everyone gets off course. Redirecting the class is key, but we do not have to do wrong to get attention or be noticed. These types of behaviors from students cause some schools to develop school expectations.

I noticed some schools displayed signs with

expectations or tolerance codes in front of the school and in classrooms. These were written instructions on noise or voice levels that were acceptable and unacceptable behaviors in the school to maintain a safe environment. The noise or voice level charts used a number system from zero to five to rank acceptable noise levels in classrooms and throughout the school. For example, zero – meant no talking or voices off, one – meant whispering or low voices, two – meant talking low, and so on … up to five or six. By enforcing the noise or voice level charts, school were teaching children how to respect others who are learning as well as keeping them on task while in the building.

Sometimes, I was not sure if any of these systems worked based on the behavior of the students in some schools. However, if it worked for them, then it worked. But, if did not work, then it was time to change. I do know that the students care about keeping points for their behavior, opposed to losing points.

Why is it so important for you to teach your children and get involved with them? It is important because you are teaching them how to get along with others later in life. I talked to parents about their expectations and shared ideas with them.

First, I would ask parents did they notice the school's expectations or rules? You would not believe how many parents have their children in school all year without knowing or understanding the school's expectations. No matter how many times the schools sent home newsletters, handouts, sent emails, or made calls, some parents still never heard or saw the expectations. No fault finding here, just an observation. So, if parents had not seen rules, I would share them or inform the school that the parent needed that information. Here it goes again, communication is a two-way street!

The key to being the best parent is making sure you

get all the information as well as allowing someone to help you receive it. You would not believe how many times I came across parents who shared with me that they did not see or get needed information. Again, we are not going there, but know changes are happening. You are changing and the school system is changing too. I shared with parents that once they saw and understood the expectations, it is their responsibility to help their children to fully understand those expectations or rules. Yes, some teachers may share and believe that you received the information, and some will not. You are an excellent parent! Ensure your child understands the rules and expectations. So, when your child gets off task, you can check the expectations and rules and know what was not followed. For the record, this is how miscommunication happens when parents accuse teachers, the principal, or other school staff of not providing information. It is also noticeably clear when teachers accuse parents too. Make sure you have all the information you need to inform your child and communicate with the school.

Secondly, I made sure the teacher, principal, and other school staff have issued communication in all the ways (letter, email, text, voice mail) to ensure parents received the expectations and rules for their school. I have seen it over and over. No matter how many school meetings I attended, everyone said the same thing, "… But we did inform them." And, some do … but somehow this communication always got muddled or lost.

Knowing the expectations and rules, especially helps when there is a substitute in the classroom. Even if teachers left a full-page book of every student and sometimes pictures of where each student sits, the substitute still does not know your child. They will know the behavior and some of the games played by students, but again, this is extremely important to ensuring your child is fully equipped and familiar with the rules.

So, to you the parent, once you contact the school, set the bar high. Develop high expectations for you and your child. Despite what others think of you, you climb the ladder. Sometimes climbing the ladder can be lonely but do it anyway. Everyone could be looking at you and wondering why you are different. You are different because you expect the best. You are different because God made you highly favored and wonderful. What are your expectations for you and your child? What are your expectations upon enrolling your child at a school or homeschool?

Here are some expectations you should set when you are stuck in the house or in the school building:

Tip #1: Teach your child to respect themselves, you, other adults, and youth/peers

Tip #2: Teach your child how to sit quietly while someone is talking or presenting

Tip #3: Teach your child how to wait and listen to

others before speaking

Tip #4: Teach your child how to keep their room clean by picking up after themselves and not littering

Tip #5: Teach your child how to love themselves, you, their family, and others

Tip #6: Teach your child to appreciate you, others, themselves, and life

Tip #7: Teach your child to read and love reading, writing, and math

Tip #8: Teach your child to learn new about new culture, people, and nations

Tip #9: Teach your child to love God

Tip #10: Teach your child to help others and volunteer in places other than your home

You can add to this list of expectations. These expectations can be used at home, school, or wherever you go. Since many places are closed right now or continuing to slowly open, exercise these expectations via virtual video. Take virtual field trips and put what you learned to practice. You can still practice going to the grocery store for essentials.

Here are a few more expectations to add to the list:

Tip #11: Teach your child when to raise their hand for help or to answer questions

Tip #12: Teach your child when to speak up and how to speak to adults and others

Tip #13: Teach your child how to walk in a straight line for school or anywhere else

Tip #14: Teach your child how to obey God first, you, speakers, guests, and the laws.

Tip #15: Teach your child how to follow directions and rules the first time

Tip #16: Teach your child how and when to turn off the cellphone

Tip #17: Teach your child when to keep all toys and

electronic gadgets at home

Tip #18: Teach your child how to keep their hands and feet to themselves

Tip #19: Teach your child how to be nice and positive with others

Tip #20: Teach your child the importance of education

Tip #21: Teach your child good language skills, not foul language, and how to speak to others

Tip #22: Teach your child to value and appreciate life

Tip #23: Teach your child how to play respectfully with others

Tip #24: Teach your child to not talk back to adults

Some of these expectations are what you will see in most schools. However, you are responsible for ensuring that your child understands them and uses them. Children are always watching adults and their surroundings. When they see wrong, they assume that it is correct. Teach them and correct wrong behaviors.

Lastly, working and parenting at home can be chaotic, but it does not have to be. It should be as simple as making a sandwich. I once taught a writing lesson on making a sandwich. I will use a simple peanut butter and jelly sandwich example.

Here are your ingredients:

Wheat or white sliced bread, bun, roll, it could even be pita bread

Jelly (my favorite)

Peanut butter

Butter knife

Plate

First, gather all your ingredients, bread, jelly, and peanut butter. Second, place to slices of bread on the plate, then place jelly on one side of the bread and then peanut butter on the other slice. Third, put both slices together and eat with milk or juice. Simple. This is what it is like when you take what you learned and put it together with new information, even if you heard some or all the information before. Take what you have and build on it. There, you did it! You did it! Once you get going, you will find that you can do anything. Some ideas and projects are simple, others are difficult, but in the end, you can do it.

Again, when you are stuck in the house, you must develop a schedule, learn to communicate better, and create lasting expectations that go beyond home and school.

Chapter Three

You Are One in a Million

You did it! You won! You are the Best! Girl, you got this! Man, you got this! Every parent would love to hear these words. What did you do? You made it to this chapter. "Yay!" No really, you did it! You made it as a concerned parent. This chapter is about how I appreciate you. Your children will appreciate you too for taking the time, extra time to guide, nurture, care, and love them.

After coming from the "Pause" of the Coronavirus Pandemic (COVID-19), it is now your time to excel as a better parent and show your child that you are in charge. Though times seem bleak, it is still your time and season to shine. So far, I shared information about scheduling, planning, and helping your child excel in school. It may seem like loads of work, but as you continue to keep your goals in front, you will make it to the finish line

I always appreciated parents who showed love and support for their children. However, if you could not support your child, but somehow found the strength to seek answers and found someone to guide you to them, then you made it. You are appreciated too. This is about you. You are one in a million! Now, I would get upset with you if you absolutely did not care and did not want to help your child. Got it!

This is about empowering you to keep going, even if you are successful at navigating the school system. For those of you who struggle and have no clue where to start in navigating the school, I want you to become empowered. Each one, teach one. In the end, you will see that you can do it! You will hear those words ringing in your ears while in you are sleep, "You did it!" If you did not know, you are your own cheerleader. Your team consists of you as parents, guardians, grandparents, and your children. Go team!!! By the way, teaching children is a must! As a teacher and educator, I cannot always be there to hold your hand, walk you through it, and cheer you on, but you are one in a million. I believe it …and I believe in you.

I must share my educational soap box. It is good smelling soap too. I call it my educational zone

Education has always been a significant part of my life. As it should be a huge part in you and your children's lives. Everyone grew up with a different outlook on education. I grew up in a strict Christian household, where home, church, and school were the only outlets in my life. Even though, my parents took my siblings and I to church, we still had Bible study every day – 365 days a year. I know you are thinking, "Oh my LORD, Jesus! Whew, glad that wasn't me!" That is okay. Growing up, I wished it were not me either, but it was. As a matter of fact, I am so glad that my parents taught me how to read the Bible, how to develop a relationship with God, and how to pray. They were one in a million. See, I told you, it is all about being you. You are the parent; you make the rules … just make good ones.

Unfortunately, in many cultures, education does not come easily. But through the grace of God, some have overcome educational hurdles. Several sayings encourage us, such as, "Education is our goal" … "Fight for what is right" … "Knowledge is power." Perhaps these phrases continue to ring true to remind people the value of stability.

Learning is an experience we all have. Whether we learn good or bad information, we are learning something. It does not matter whether you received a great deal or a little information, we are in a time and century where learning is at our fingertips. The internet, new technology gadgets, workshops, and programs have allowed for no excuses.

Education is a goal no matter what struggle you are in. We all learn differently and at our own pace. You do not have to achieve the highest degree to show everyone how intelligent you are but get all you can and store it in your mind and on paper too. So, you may be thinking, Ms. Jackson, just because you have it, that does not mean I can easily get it too. Yes, you can! Remember, you are one in a million.

As you embark upon the ending of this summer break, you may be preparing for that last family vacation, while others will focus on buying school supplies. If you have not found the time to develop your goals for the school year, review what I have provided later in this chapter.

This is the best time to develop better working relationships with your child, their teachers, principals, other school staff, and parent advocates. Once school is in session, you have many opportunities to make known your concerns and values to strengthen the school atmosphere.

Classroom observation is good. The good thing about showing up is you can see your child and you are able to see where they need help. You will also see other children perform as well. Observing your child at school is different than when they are at home. Watching them helps you make better decisions at home or wherever you go. When we observe students, we take part in addressing emotional, intellectual, and cultural issues.

May 25, 2020, in Minneapolis, Minnesota was a clear traumatic moment that shed light on systemic racism that seemed geared only at African American men and women. That murdering of George Floyd at the knee of a Minneapolis police office sparked an outcry throughout several cities in America, which called for major observation and discussion, especially in the school system.

Throughout my years of teaching, there were several special education students mainstreamed in my class who had Individual Educational Plans (IEP). These plans meant they either had one on one support or could work independently with little support.

I saw a rise in special education, especially among African American boys. They were being labeled as having Emotional Behavior Disorder (EBD) or Attention Deficit Disorder (ADD). Though labeling students varies from state to state, there is still a spike in several school districts across America. Labels, especially negative ones, do not help anyone.

As educators, we must change the paradox from continuously labeling and seeing African American young boys as poster children for negative behavior boys, see them as young men growing into becoming kings. From my observation, these young boys need to be active every 10 minutes. It was hard for them to sit through a lesson for 10 minutes before finding something else to do or disrupt class.

There are some children who after sitting for a long while will work in their own space. Sometimes they are distracted by too much going on in the class or distracted because there were too many children in the class. This is where observation helps you as the parent. You can see for yourself how your child responds in class. While I was a teacher and advocate, I met with parents who came in screaming, hollering, or just simply quiet not knowing where to begin.

As an advocate, I received a call from a parent after their child's teacher was absent from school one day. They shared with me that their child was blamed for something that they should not have been blamed for. Nevertheless, I listened to this parent, who confidently said to me, "Not my child". It was tough to say to parents, that sometimes their children could cause mishap. Yet, I listened intently. Of course, there were various reasons those situations arise which include: lack of instruction, boredom, and anger. In some classrooms, having the special education and regular teacher instructing students caused confusion.

But, have no fear, we are all learning, there is a way

to improve any situation. By the way, substitute teachers are like new teachers working with your child. They meet your child for the first time with no knowledge of your child's behaviors or needs. Most substitute teachers are not used to working with students with special needs and have no idea what makes your child special.

Dominque was labeled with EBD. He bullied other students and felt he deserved all the attention. He kept bothering Phillip, another student in class. Unfortunately, they both hit and bothered other students. Dominque had an IEP that explained that he got bored quickly in class. The key for the teacher or guest teacher was always to keep him active. The result, Dominque's educational plan was set up so that he could feel successful academically while working on his actions

Face it parents, you are tired and stressed too. When it comes to helping your child at school or with their classwork, you are at your wit's end. And now more than ever, you are more stressed because you must help your child at home since the school building was closed while you were still working from home. It does not seem fair. It always looked easy when the teacher had them, but now you have them.

Some schools do a wonderful job teaching and helping parents understand their child, yet others are not as successful. When it comes to the needs of your child in special education, some school staff listen to you and others only seem to help you because they want to get paid. They are and are not willing to show you how to teach your child with disabilities. You want the teachers and school to treat your child well.

Clearly, reviewing the expectations and rules of the school or classroom at the beginning of school is crucial for a successful year. Once you have spoken to your child about the expectations, it is now their responsibility to follow the rules. I will add that some behaviors are due to being bored in the classroom. Sometimes the lessons are long, boring, and not interesting. Parents should communicate with teachers to ensure their lessons are valuable and beneficial so that their child has an interest in learning. If you have a child in special education, I want to offer some suggestions of what to do at an Individualized Educational Plan (I.E.P.) Meeting in the classroom.

Absolutely know your child's IEP:

Here is what to do at an Individualized Educational Plan (I.E.P.) Meeting:

Tip #1: Make sure you receive a meeting notice and then show up at the meeting

Tip #2: Become familiar and absolutely know your child's I.E.P.

Tip #3: Know who is on the I.E.P. team

Tip #4: During the meeting, listen attentively to everyone, take notes, and observe body language

Tip #5: Go over the plan so that you are clear and

understand it

Tip# 6: Ask questions, offer suggestions, and improvements to the plan

Tip #7: Hold yourself and everyone accountable to the plan you all decide on

Tip #8: Check to see if the plan is working, if not, make changes

Tip #9: It is a process, so make sure you follow through and willing to wait

Tip #10: Set the next meeting and place it on your calendar – most I.E.P. meetings happen once or twice a year

Another job assignment for you is checking-in with your child's classroom. Make sure this is a goal you establish at the beginning of the school year, so the teacher knows that you will show up and support them while checking-in on your child. You can always suggest ideas to the teacher so that your child stays on task or at least focused on the assignment. If you find your child is not focused, I suggest having them count blank sheets, organize the room, go for a walk, or write sentences. Your child may need special projects or simply need more work.

Here are some ideas to help your child behave better in the classroom:

Tip #1: Give your child smaller assignments and tasks that take a short time to complete.

Tip #2: Ensure your child understands what you expect of them and then support the school in fostering good behavior.

Tip #3: Find what your child likes and help incorporate those fun ideas into the lesson

Tip #4: Suggest other ways your child can learn and get the same information especially if they have lots of energy. We have learned a lot about you and your child being number one! We have explored being a part of a special education meetings and observing and helping in the classroom. Right now, I want to shift your attention to understanding what to do before choosing a school. If your child is placed in special education, you must properly enroll them to a school that meets and exceeds their needs. Throughout the rest of this chapter, I discuss and share suggestions on navigating, visiting, enrolling, meeting with a potential school.

Choosing the right school for your child can be tedious. You may feel like you do not have any experiences or skills, but you are influential. You may be feeling rejected, but when you sit back and look at the picture, you are still one in a million. Besides, rejection, will happen. When it comes, take it, get up, and move forward. Once you choose a school, there are ways that you can navigate the school.

Here are five tips you can use when choosing a school for your child:

Tip #1:

Locating the right school for your child is like looking for a new house. You want to find the best school where your child will be housed at least 6 to 8 hours a day. Finding a school is as important as the day you had your child and brought them home from the hospital. You want that same warmth, kind, and loving atmosphere. Make a visit to your child's school to meet the principal and staff. While you are there check out the atmosphere, the other staff, how children are being treated, and how you are being treated. This can happen anytime throughout the year, but especially do it before you decide on changing schools.

I met with families who enrolled at a school and weeks or months later were not happy with their choice. In the end, it is not just finding the right school, enrolling your child, and leaving them to fend for themselves. It is you, the parent, taking delight in knowing that your child is in capable hands that you picked with care. And, then you continue to care for your child while they attend the school through your involvement.

Tip #2:

Once you have found the right school, what do you do next? When meeting the principal and teachers, let them know what you are looking for and what you want for your child. You do not have to let them know all about your child at the time, but it may be good to say something small. Meet the teachers and the staff.

Tip #3:

Once you meet the principal and teachers, continue to prepare your child academically and socially. Find out about resources that will help your child through the school year by researching on the web, the local library, and/or other agencies.

Tip #4:

Stay connected with your child's school throughout the year. Show up at conferences, book fairs, and other events.

Tip #5:

Make yourself available. When enrolling your child in school, sign up for a few meetings here and there. This is simple enough for some parents, but not others. However, you can do this. You have that parent power in you. Pace yourself when teaching and working with your child. There is no one better than you who can do that. You are number one in their life. Even if you do not know what to do, seek the answers. Being present is key. You may not have the professional training or home training, but you can do this.

Navigating the school

Many parents have a tough time choosing a school for their child. They cannot decide whether to attend a school close to home or away from home.

Two big questions that I mainly heard while working with parents was what school is best for my child and what do I do once they are enrolled? Over time, I have been asked which is better, public school, private school, charter school, or home school? I like them all and I believe they all benefit children.

The real issue, then and now, is what you will are you willing to do as the parent. You are your child's first teacher. It does not matter what school or teacher you choose. You must participate in your child's educational journey. So, when asked about which is a better choice, inner city or suburban? Again, it is up to you. The real question is how much work are you willing to put in for your child? Yes, it is work. Parenting is work. To accomplish something, one must work. There are some similarities and differences that I have seen and learned from inner city and suburban schools:

Inner city schools seemed to dwell more on rules. They have their share of more disruptive students, enroll more low-income students, have little use of technology, more students of color, and for some inner-city schools, lower academic expectations for African American students. At the same time, there are some great teachers and staff members at these schools who will instruct your child in the right direction.

Suburban schools typically are newer buildings, allow more freedom, have majority white students and staff, with a few other races. There is an emphasis on art education, updated technology, and updated lunch machines. Suburban schools traditionally have fewer disruptive students, higher expectations for students and special education staff and students sometimes treated a little better. Again, they may or may not have a staff with a mindset to openly accept your child. Of course, you will have to check out these schools for yourself. As we dive into what you want, look at schools as if it was a menu board. Know what you want! What are you looking for in a school? One way to look at this is like a restaurant menu board.

On the menu:

School size

The school faculty and staff – Are they pleasant and helpful?

Culture – if culture is important to you, what culture are you looking for? (All Asian/Hmong, East African, African American, Hawaiian, or Native American). With an emphasis on culture, ultimately, it is about learning about the cultures to work and live with them.

As a parent, meeting with teachers and other support staff is the best thing to do. When you get involved, your child has better success. Stay focused on what is best for you and your child. Being the number one parent means your child can succeed in school. When you meet with the teachers, you can see what is best for your child.

Questions you should ask when meeting with school administrators:

Tip #1: What are your expectations for my child, other children, and the school?

Tip #2: Where and how can I help the school?

Tip #3: How can I help my child grow and succeed?

Once you have met with the teacher, principals, and other staff, it is beneficial to start developing working relationships with them so that they get to know you and your child. This will help you succeed.

Building working relationships again is very key. Once you enroll your child to a school, it is time to build working relationships with the staff. Check out some of the tips above. You want to know the staff and make sure they know your child. This is a must. This continues to be a big problem in some schools. Help the school learn about your child in all the ways that you can. This is about you making a difference, getting up and fulfilling your duties as a parent. Not many parents will follow through, but you can be the example. What your child is looking for is help and support from you while you are getting help from the teacher. I know some students do not want their parents to show up at school. I get it! But your presence is essential to your child's success.

Along with helping build relationships, you are also partnering with the school. Just like other organizations, churches, and non-profits partners. Partnering and working with your child's schools is essential in making a difference and enhances your child's education. In other words, remain determined and persistent throughout the process

Here are five tips to participate with your child's school:

Tip #1: Find ways to participate in the classroom

and at school events. For example, the month of February is Black History and I Love to Read Month. Become a guest reader in your child's class or show a storybook to the students during an online class session.

Tip #2: Advocate for your child. Basically, this means attending conferences, I.E.P., meetings, and planning meetings at the school. There are several workshops and parental classes to help in this area. I suggest having a plan, knowing your plan, and showing up to present your plan.

Tip #3: Model what you want to see. Be the positive role model for your child. No school likes a loud parent sitting in the office breathing hot and yelling uncontrollably. If this is you, believe me, some schools have radars and know when you are coming. Some secretaries know your voice on the phone, your walk, and car color even before you pull into the parking lot. They hear you coming from down the street! Instead of being negative, always have a "winning attitude" when meeting with the school.

Now I am not saying, "dance around the bush!" I am saying, know why you are showing up, have legitimate complaints, and represent yourself well. It is important to note, some school personnel are encouraged to shut your complaints down.

They really do not know you are a winning parent. Also, it will be good practice to check in with friends if you face one of those hot issues with your children. Know your rights, know that you have rights, and have the right plan. After all, you want the best for your child.

Tip #4: Articulate what you want. Write down your plan before springing into action.

Tip #5: Prepare your child for school. Take visits to the library or other resources to get help.

Goal setting:

What is a goal? A goal is a statement or purpose for fulfilling something. What are your goals? When making short and long-term goals, it allows you to see what you are aiming for and obtaining that result.

How to Choose the Right Goals for your child:

Tip #1: Perseverance. Keep going and fighting for your child even when you get tired.

Tip #2: Making the most of the year

Tip #3: Creating a daily activity log

Tip #4: Develop a family guide. Plan for you and your family when tough situations arise throughout the school year. For example, what would you do if your child is suspended or accused of wrongdoing? Discuss with your family what your expectations are, hopefully those events will not happen, but at least mention and write down your plan of action.

A Biblical Scripture that references goals is

Philippians 3:14 KJV, I press toward the mark for the prize of the high calling of God in Christ Jesus. Another reference from First Timothy 1:5 KJV, Now the end of the commandment is charity out of a pure heart, and of a good conscience, and of faith unfeigned. Both speak to continuing the race in love even when you are ready to quit. No matter how many times your voice is not heard at school or your child is ignored, stay the course. The more you press in, the better the results.

Tip #5: Learn quotes from notable and influential people. For example, "It is easier to build strong children than to repair broken men." Fredrick Douglass

Here is an example of a letter that you can use when making goals for your child with the school:

Memo:

To: All interested parties (the teacher, principal, others working with your child):

Re: Goals for my child

These are the goals that I have established for my son or daughter, as they continue at your school. To achieve these goals during this school year, my child will:

Recognize ten sight words a week and achieve 80-100%.

Spell at least 10 words each week during the spelling test to achieve 80%-100%.

Secure math skills needed to obtain at least 75%. -100%

Move from being dependent on the teacher to working independently, mastering 100% of his work. My child will be attentive in class and will stay on task

My child will work in group with other students and succeed

In addition, I will increase my communications

through phone calls, e-mails, conferences, and meetings. All parties will agree to e-mail on a weekly or monthly basis to ensure success of my child.

Of course, that is one example, but you can design and develop your own goal chart to make it work for you. Developing a plan along with your goals helps you remain clear about what your assignment is. Setting goals allows you to see and set your future accomplishments, whether they are short or long. More examples include the one listed below. By writing down goals you are making no more excuses.

Here are more goals:

Goal #1: Share your expertise and ideas

Goal #2: Volunteer with homework

Goal #3: Start a Parent's Club/group

Goal #4: Start a newsletter

Goal #5: Recruit other parents – get the word out to school districts

Goal #6: Read to children and support their activities

Goal #7 Conduct meetings with other parents

What is it that you want to do with your life? Spend some time writing down short and long terms goals. Write down ideas and goals about how you will help at school and at home. Make a list of goals for the next 3-5 years. List your lifetime goals this school year and years to come if your child is in school. What is it that you need to do to accomplish your goals? Share what you will do today, tomorrow, next week, next month, and throughout the year. If you are excited about the school year and our ready for it to begin, write down your ideas for an exciting school year. You will have a fun filled exciting year once you write those goals. Goals help you stay on track. They give you something to look at that will remind you of what you are doing. Make those goals and have fun.

No More Excuses:

We all make excuses for not doing something. You may have made excuses, but I want you to decree now, no more excuses! We often make excuses and procrastinate when it comes to doing something important. What type of excuses have you made for not achieving what you want to accomplish? I am going to share with you five ways goals help you avoid making excuses.

In many schools today there is a lack of parental involvement and support. Many parents have many excuses as to why they cannot participate at their child's school. Now some of those reasons may be legitimate such as their work schedule, no transportation, no babysitter, or daycare, and just simply no time. But I am here to share that you can find ways to participate and become more involved with your child in school. I call these the five P's. I want you to write these down.

The First P is Plan.

Planning is something we do all the time, whether

we organize our plans or not. We plan for both positive and negative events in our lives. When we want something or we must be somewhere important, we will plan for it. I know you are thinking, "No, I don't plan life, it just happens." But we plan for birthday parties, favorite meals, what to buy when shopping, and where to eat out? Let us face it, we plan whether we want to admit it or not. When I worked as a parent advocate, parents came to me for enrolling their child in school, I often sat down with them and helped them create a school year plan. This will help in your child's success throughout the school year. I would share with parents to mark off at least five days on the calendar throughout the school year to visit their child's school. The first thing that I would hear is, "Oh, I don't have time to visit the school that many times during the year" or "I won't be able to get time off."

Now, I realize some parents may not have a lot of time off. At least, choose 3 to5 days throughout the school year, between September and June, to visit the school. If you plan right, you could participate beyond five days. Plan those days with your child before the beginning of the school. Excellent time to plan is during the summer when school is out. You have quality time to sit down with your child and plan their entire school year. It takes time to implement plans, but you can do it. It is never too late plan.

The Second P is Participate.

Many of us like to participate in our favorite activities, groups, and even volunteer with our favorite charity groups. Participation is a way to show your support and concern for the school.

The Third P is Pay Attention.

Sometimes it seems as if we pay attention more to the negative news reports than the good reports. Paying attention to your child's education, hobbies, and activities shows how attentive you are.

The Fourth P is Persistence.

To get something accomplished you must be persistent. This means when you want your child to do his or her best in school, you must consistently check their learning. Spend nights at home practicing new vocabulary words with them. Allow them to read their favorite book as well as read challenging books to enhance their reading vocabulary. Allow your child to see themselves as a success. Create affirmations that they can recite daily. Affirmations help you move up the leader as well as encourage you.

The Fifth P is Patience.

Some of you may have heard the saying, "Patience is a virtue." In most anything that we do in life, we must wait. As adults, we wait on paychecks that come either every week, every other week, or monthly. When you learn to wait, you will feel better about making a difference in your child's life. Despite the type of neighborhood or ethnic background you come from, you can make a difference at your child's school.

Parents often want to blame the teachers and the schools for their child's lack of education. Teachers often blame the parents for lack of knowledge and participation. This sentiment is felt in many schools across the country, but it takes two or the whole village to help raise a child. School and teachers become secondary parents.

Above all, learning how to navigate the school system, learning how to participate, enroll, and develop working relationships confirms your commitment to your child's growth.

Chapter Four

Breaking Point

Over the years, I heard parents say, "Teachers have too many breaks! It may look that way, but your child is still in school more than you think. Some parents and teachers are at the boiling and breaking point. "Help me, I need break! I need a break!" We all need a break. Yes, I get it! You need a break. There comes a time when everyone needs a break. Amazingly, the Coronavirus pandemic became the new surprised school break.

The key to getting that break, is scheduling that break. We all yearn for a break from time to time. Breaks help us to rest, relax, rejuvenate, and get back up again. Whether it is you or your children, you both need a break. If this is you, then this chapter is for you. You were screaming, "Help me, I need a break!" Well, help is here.

Whether it is a minor or major break you need, or if

you are at that breaking point of falling out, I recommend finding someone to talk too or finding something constructive to do. Breaks tend to interrupt our lives or the flow of something. It is like the example I shared in chapter one of driving down a long road at night and a deer suddenly jumps out at your vehicle. It can also represent a time when you were going along your merry way and suddenly, boom, you receive miserable news that causes you to stop. We do plan for breaks in our lives, but sometimes breaks show up unexpectedly. This is a part of life.

We have all dealt with a breaking point at some point in our lives. If you have not experienced that breaking point, keep living. Face it, we feel the breaking point during the best and worst of times. It is most troublesome when you are at the breaking point and do not know what to do. The best way to build and move on from there is to recognize it and move on.

Remember in chapter two, *I Do Not Have Time*, you learned how to create a schedule. Making a schedule allows you to see where to take your break and makes sure it happens. If you have not made that schedule, quickly jot down a schedule right now. At least put down numbers one to three and fill it in later.

Speaking of breaks, I remember one time I had an easy job assignment. I had to sit in the lunchroom and monitor students and then make sure students cleaned up after lunch. This school assignment was a break from being in the classroom. There were also moments when I needed a break too.

On several occasions while teaching, I had students moving from school to school during the middle of the school year. Sometimes the move happened a few weeks after school started, sometimes in December during the winter break, sometimes in March, or even May before school was to end in June. Though it was not clear sometimes of why families moved, it hindered students from succeeding and remaining on grade level with their classmates.

This negative impact is a breaking point for parents. It is difficult for parents when they are up against the demands of life. Sadly, I have seen some of these students leave and then show up again the following school year with the same mindset. Basically, they continued to struggle and remained in the same place they were in when they left. Before I share some tips on how to get passed some negative breaking points, I want to share some more examples.

Another example of a negative breaking point came when I was teaching a student who could not read well. This student was excited about learning and wanted to know how they were doing. As much as they enjoyed learning, they were not comprehending spelling words. I would give a spelling list at the beginning of the week and have students go over it. I would give a pre-test on Thursday to see who studied. If they passed the test on Thursday, they did not have to take the text on Friday. Well, this student had trouble comprehending the sounds of the words. They were excited about writing and words, so I thought they were doing well. But they were not spelling the words correctly.

When I mentioned it to the parent, the parent felt that the words that I gave were too hard and above their child's comprehension level, and claimed I was not acknowledging their child's difficulty of learning the words. The parent also shared with me their way of teaching phonics and sight words to their child. This proves the importance of creating a schedule and time with your child. Now, I know, some parents do not have time. We addressed this in chapter two. However, I am suggesting that you make time. You could put this book to the side and make a schedule right now. Schedules help you keep appointments and have a better life for you and your child.

Over the years, I watched new teachers start the first day of school and at the end of the day, they decided, teaching was not for them. They rushed out of the education arena. And then there were teachers who taught through the end of the 1st week of school. At least they made it to Friday and then made that leap. Then, there were times when teachers made it to the Thanksgiving holiday and did not return for the last few weeks before winter break. The most common time when teachers made their exit was during winter break. It seemed to be a better time to escape without the children or staff making you feel guilty. Yes, it is for teachers to quit at any time. I could not walk away from my students. I was too far in the game.

From the beginning of my early years until now, the thought of just leaving was not in me. I did not care what type of situations I faced, it was not enough for me to cave in and walk away. After all, this was the career I wanted. So yes, there were some significant moments that could have or did bring me to a breaking point, but only enough to take that break and then move forward.

After my first year of teaching, I thought, "Oh wow, these young people don't want to learn." That year was filled with students who did not push to succeed. It seemed to be a year where students and parents were coming to this idea that school just was not important enough.

By the time I reached my third year, I was teaching 1st graders. I had a fellow teacher who had a student in her class who screamed loudly. The child was extremely loud and would cry for at least two hours –yes, two hours! This could have been a breaking point for that teacher. It was only the first week of school and this child screamed every day.

By the time we had our team meeting, the teacher who had this child in her class was ready to give up. Our meeting was to help brainstorm ideas on how to help the student and the teacher. Well, you know how this goes, the set up, and then the news. After our meeting, my principal came to me the next day and asked me to take this student. I immediately said yes. I said yes because I thought that was what I was supposed to do … help. The student was placed in my class the following week.

My breaking point seemed to come before and after this student. For weeks before this student was placed in my class, I was hearing him screaming, and now he was screaming in my class. What was I to do? Quit? I was getting tired of his screaming. I started to rethink if I made the right decision. Could I back out and return him back to his original class? I was breaking and I was not sure if that was okay for me as the teacher.

The critical part to recognize is that this situation was in my hands. I had the opportunity to make change. Or as many would say, take lemons and make lemonade.

No matter what I thought, this interruption in my third year seemed right on time. I was breaking, but I knew God set it up. All I could do was pray. Yes, pray! I put this child on my church prayer list and kept praying myself.

It was mid-October and this young boy continued to scream. He decreased his cry time from two hours down to about an hour and 45 minutes. As I kept praying during my own time at home, I noticed this young boy's crying and screaming was changing. He was still screaming, but not for two hours. Now it was December, that moment and time when some teachers decide it is good time to run and not return.

By December, this young boy's crying was now down to one hour. He was getting better and getting used to being in my class. He was trusting me as his teacher. As he was changing, I was changing. The thought of breaking was fading. Once I recognized that I was breaking, I learned to stop, examine where I was, and keep going.

After my rest from winter break, I was ready to tackle this situation and defeat what was trying to attack and break me. I was ready, more than ready, for this young boy's challenge.

By January, the student's crying continued to decrease. It was amazing to watch him get used to his surroundings and finally feel loved. I celebrated the changes I saw in him. I was happy to know that my other students were exceptionally well-behaved throughout the months when the child was having screaming tantrums. God had sent the right six-year-old "angels" students that year.

While this young boy was in my class, the social worker and special education director had been working on having him tested for special education. Since the day he arrived, and exhibited screaming tantrums, they knew he was not placed in the right school. However, it took months for paperwork to be filled out and another school to be chosen for him. I was on board with helping him succeed in the right school.

The time had come for this second breaking point. I had become attached to helping and seeing this young boy change. In March, his screaming tantrums went from an hour and 45 minutes to 1 hour, down to five or less minutes. Yes, in March he was screaming for 5 minutes or less.

Following one of his meetings, a decision was made to relocate him to another school. He was eligible for special education. For me, that meant excitement and joy. He will get the help he needed, but now it presented another breaking point for me. I was losing one of my students. I was feeling lost and hopeless.

I had spent the past seven months stressed, frustrated, upset, yet happy and excited that all that work made me a better teacher. Letting him go was not easy. I was not able to separate the labor of love with focusing on managing my class. The decision was final. He was scheduled to leave and not return to my classroom after spring break. I noticed that my breaking point, humbled me even when I was upset and out of sorts.

Right now, you are already ahead of the game. You are making progress by getting past the breaking point and putting together a schedule. Again, using the breaks throughout the school year and not just waiting for the summer, though that helps you and your child get ahead. There are countless opportunities throughout the school year before summer, winter, or spring break.

Although, I agree summer break is probably the best time to either take your break alone or with your child. It also is that time to discover and tackle old and new challenges. Take time to look back at the school year, and then prepare for a next year. The power is in your hands.

Most schools provide school calendars at the beginning of the school year with scheduled conferences, meetings, and days off for students so that parents will know when to show up at school and when their child stays home.

The calendar outlines teacher professional days, Thanksgiving, winter break, spring break, and summer break. As a matter of fact, if you regularly get information or newsletters from your child's school, you will see the school calendar.

So, there are many opportunities to take a break throughout the school year and spend quality time with your children. Use these moments to your advantage. Choose wisely. It is up to you how you spend those breaks with your children. Make a schedule and then find time to do something while on the break.

Remember it is about you and your precious child. Again, whether you home school or send your child to a school building, find time to schedule that break. Taking a break does not just mean, sit back, watch tv, and do nothing, well, it could. The point here is, taking that quality time and doing something useful and meaningful for you and your child. It means continuing to do something fun and exciting. In some ways, having those breaks, breaks up the negative and positive impact of children's lives.

If you teach your child to disrespect adults and curse (use foul language) then expect teachers/educators at the school to frequently call and visit you. And if they do not, then it is because they do not want to bother or teach your child. The teacher is not teaching bad behaviors at school, but basic math, English, writing, spelling, computer skills, speaking, and learning communication skills for life. Like teachers, you can help get an early start in making good choices and teaching your child.

Negative Impact:

There are some schools and even teachers who see negative behaviors in both parents and the students they teach, even if they do not possess those negative behaviors. One negative impact that children experience in school is not comprehending materials from reading, math, or writing. Some children with several dynamics in their lives, have a hard time focusing on lessons in the classroom. As a parent, it is important to make that schedule and take advantage of those breaks. You are ensuring that your child is not only ready for the classroom, but ready for the next grade level, school, and/or district.

Earlier this year, many of us were at a breaking point. However, this unlikely moment, though it seemed unbearable, presented an occasion that gave us time. Everyone in America and a few countries surrounding America dealt with the "Stay at Home Order" due to the Coronavirus pandemic. Some parents had a hard time staying in the house with their children, while others were engulfed with activities and projects. I am sure it was not easy being home with your child while working full time.

Some of you had to juggle teaching school lessons, working online, babysitting, cooking, cleaning the house, and keeping everyone's lives in order.

However, looking back at those months, hopefully you learned more about yourself and your child. And, if you did not have that time to do so, sit down and examine what was going on. Then find creative ways to get through to enjoy this time at home.

Here are some ways that you can take a break and have fun with your child in the house:

Tip #1: Spotlight each other by writing thank you notes

Tip #2: Write a story, or play interactive learning games

Tip #3: Cook your favorite foods and snacks

Tip #4: Play games on the internet, or design new games

Tip #5: Learn new dance moves or watch exercise

videos

Tip #6: Take a break and learn about your family tree

Tip #7: Create and set up camp or imaginary places in the house

Tip #8: Use social media sites such as You-Tube, Instagram, and Facebook

Whatever you decide, make it fun. You want your child to see that you are with them in learning both academically and socially. It is about coming together, sharing, and being with each other. The mission seems impossible, but you can do it. If you are not sure where to start, start with what you know. You are the expert in your house. Sure, you may feel that you are not talented or gifted like others, but you are you. You can perform tasks that allow you to be praised by your children. The key is to begin. Once you have discovered your breaking point, it is time to look for the positive ways to counter them and excel to a new level.

Positive Impact

On the other hand, some schools and teachers do a wonderful job communicating with parents. The most positive impact you have with your child is being there for them. When your child sees that you are there in everything they do, they are excited to be fully supported. Some children see it and will acknowledge it, others will not and continue searching for it.

Calling all parents! This is all a part of playing the game. Valuable lessons come when families take the time to understand each other and what is around them.

By getting involved, your child is noticing the positive impact of the support you are giving. You will know what is important for your child. At the same know what you are getting involved in. You are ahead of the game. You may not be an expert, but you can handle what you are capable of structuring. Despite where you are, allow your confidence to rise. You are a diamond.

Again, looking back over the past few months, you probably established some ideas to help you get through a breaking point. And hopefully, learned more about yourself and your child. If not, that is okay, you still have an opportunity to make a positive impact for yourself and your child.

S-u-c-c-e-s-s, a cheerleading chant I remember hearing in high school. I was not a cheerleader in high school but became a cheerleader and big fan of helping parents succeed in the classroom. Cheer Up! You will make it!

Being your own cheerleader is about ensuring that you are heard and then helping you get what you need and watching you move forward. I wanted to make sure you understood simple examples and simple solutions.

Here are some ways you can be a cheerleader for your child with their teacher:

Tip #1: Share your child's likes and dislikes

Tip #2: Alert the teacher when your child has a good or bad day.

Tip #3: Share your child's talents and gifts

Tip #4: Share your child's favorite hobbies or crafts

Tip #5: Share what subjects your child likes or does not like

When you take part and encourage ways your child works well in school, the better equipped the teacher and school will be as they work with your child. Remember, teachers are responsible for at least 15-20 students in your child's class. You are helping them by emphasizing your child's needs. As you prepare for the school year, this helps when you are working on moving from the breaking point and making a positive impact. Ultimately, you want to make sure you and your child have a successful school year.

Even if you are not sure of your parenting style, it is

okay. Many parents do not have the same parenting styles. By using your authority and implementing ideas, no matter how small or great, it shows your eagerness and the positive impact you are making. An effective parent accepts responsibility, takes the initiative and soars. You have already stepped forward and made the best decision by supporting your child and improving their education by helping them.

It is tempting to sit back and let the school and the teacher do all the work but it is your responsibility to teach your child, assume the responsibility for everything they do right or wrong, and then make sure they are succeeding. You will make a positive impact when you are focused on what is best for your child. It is time for restructuring and reevaluating how you have done things in the past. Perhaps, you may already have been extraordinary at your child's school, yet you are looking to become better? Or maybe being involved at your child's school is new for you and you have never taken the initiative to navigating the school system? To further clarify, understanding the significance of this time, positions you directly where a paradigm shift occurs.

Lastly, to make a positive impact on your child's education, give it your best. Once you have identified the concerns, plan, and act. Write it down and put it in motion. Be sure to verbalize this with your child so they fully understand and are on the same page with you and the teacher. Believe me, when children see you working for and with them, they feel special and needed. The underlying message is executing a solid successful plan.

Chapter Five

Hot as Fire!

At the time of writing this book, another young African American man was murdered by the knee of a police officer in Minneapolis, Minnesota. My first thought, "What, not again? Really!? What is happening?" There was an outrage. Interestingly, a few years earlier, while in the middle of writing my doctoral dissertation, another young African American man, Philando Castille, was also murdered at the hands of a police officer. There is a continual war of White on Black and Black and Black crime …Two of the greatest unresolved conflicts in America.

Unresolved racial issues are proof that education is crucial yet underrated. With the overlap of the Coronavirus pandemic and the plague of systemic racism it is time to reevaluate education. I found this incident interesting because, once again, my city was going through the fire.

The whole city, other cities, and the world felt this tremble.

With the Coronavirus pandemic and sparks and fires of systemic racism, the educational system will never be the same! As a teacher in the classroom, I felt it was my duty to teach life lessons and raise world concerns with my students and parents. Consequently, some students were independent thinkers. In some settings, students were given critical subjects, tackling the context of their surroundings. The quality of their education provided access and most recently gave them the confidence to achieve in school.

The opening of this chapter alluded to teaching cultural relevant material in the classroom. It is crucial that teachers in schools specifically teach the unique qualities of African American culture.[2] While culturally relevant material is being pursued, it sheds light on critical race theory.

---

[2] Billings

Teaching culturally relevant material is becoming popular in schools. It serves to allow readers to gain information far beyond what was displayed through classroom lessons. Effective teachers using culturally relevant material quickly relate to the behaviors of their students and families. Using the material connects and develops deeper relationships with families making sense and bringing balance. It reduces the stress parents may feel when provoking stories are shared in the news. A problem-solving strategy moving students and parents forward. The emphasis and approach of that strategy is to effectively use a method that benefits the learner.

Teaching culturally relevant material recognizes current issues surrounding families. A text centered on observing injustices while being intentional on seeking justice.

Hence, the murder that happened in Minneapolis could very well be like the murder of education for African

American youth. Senseless crimes, robbing and killing one another … These are all thought-provoking conversations for parents and their children.

Nevertheless, from teaching cultural relevant material to connecting parents with educational services, there are always fires that need to be put out. Like you, teachers get crazy mad too when educational misleading happens.

With regards to teaching culturally relevant information there are ways to problem solve when disagreements arrive. As a teacher, I encountered families who were misunderstood and became frustrated with the educational system. Unresolved conflict hinders growth, leaving questions on their hearts and minds.

Over the years, school communities have grown healthier with understanding various cultures, while learning new languages and ways to work with each other. However, some parents, along with their children, continue to be criticized over their cultural language and their way of life. This results in parent's personal separation from some schools.

As a parent, there are ways you can teach culturally relevant information in your child's school and iron out the misunderstandings of culture. You may be a parent sharing, or on the receiving end of learning about a new culture. Here are some tips for gathering information and exploring new cultures.

Learning from Cultures and Lifestyles:

Tip #1: Teach schools about your culture

Tip #2: Teach others about your family culture (foods, entertainment, lifestyle)

Tip #3: Host cultural events

Tip #4: Create opportunities for others to see your child's worth

Tip #5: Clarify your child's interest

Tip #6: Create discussion groups that elevate the

successes of your culture – child's needs

Distinguishing who your child is, speaks to the quality of education you seek for them. Always accentuate the positive. Misinterpretation inevitably is a key factor in labeling children, especially students of color. Seek ways to meditate and assume the greater position in re-educating others. Verbal fires start with misunderstandings and remain in that realm. Sometimes they are resolved with clarity.

For example, one parent called screaming and yelling, telling me that a school official suspended her child. She was not mad at me, but hot mad at the situation. She felt it was racist and disheartening. She was hot as fire! After getting off the phone with her, I was not sure of the miscommunication, but helped to resolve the issue. Importantly, this parent needed clarification.

Sometimes once parents have information they do not agree with, they get upset and immediately want to settle it their way, while being upset. With me by this parent's side, they were able to fully understand the situation, assess it, and make choices that worked for them. This did not happen all the time, but the key is helping parents solve heated issues when they sometimes cannot mediate for themselves. Perhaps, the real issue of the day is identifying the situation and addressing it.

Whether you are the parent that became defensive and upset or the parent with confidence, hopefully you gain important information about your child's education. Sometimes being hot helps. You can be angry and later solve a situation. Ultimately, some parents like heated discussion because it is their way of addressing their concerns and venting their frustrations.

Again, what are you doing to make a difference? Is it a positive difference at your child's school? Are you apart of the solution or the problem? Are you a winner or a loser? Whichever side you stand on, make improvements.

That being the case, let us work on what you can do.

Problem Solving/Making a Difference with the school:

Tip #1: Investigate the issue and your concerns before meeting with the school

Tip #2: Focus on one issue at a time

Tip #3: Remain calm throughout the process

Tip #4: Seek a winning solution

Tip #5: Discuss the situation

As a parent, sometimes you are having difficulties and you do not have someone to talk too. You feel alone and by yourself. It is difficult handling situations while working towards ensuring your child is doing well in school. Daily, I often prayed for my parents and my students.

You are your child's wonderful parent-teacher. You can teach your child amazing life lessons. But, no matter how exceptional you are, parenting is not easy. Many have written parenting books and manuals; all parents respond differently. You are a part of that on-going process, whether it looks like failure or success. We are always growing, learning, and maturing.

I repeat, you are your child's first teacher. When it comes to teaching and sharing tips with parents, I am "old school" … not old, but I believe in some old school teachings. I am adamant about you teaching your child the right material. Even if your cry is still, "Come get these kids!" today start your change and redirect what you say and do as you work with your child.

If you are angry, ask yourself, who are you mad at? And, why are you mad? How can you change from being mad? When did this madness begin? When I see hot, angry parents – or when they call me screaming and yelling about some issue, I put them on my prayer list. Whatever made you mad about your child's school, there are solutions. Holding on to anger will cause you to feel like you are on a top-secret assignment or on some mission that seems impossible.

Sometimes, when people are angry, they do not know what to do or say. They lash out verbally. Sometimes they react physically, but when everything boils down, the real issues come out. As a teacher and advocate, I was there to help. And I do mean help with full intent. Aside from your anger and concerns, you can still do it. Just remember, it takes time to make change and see change happen, but it can happen.

Heated situations do come up. Your first defense is to verbally express your anger and then react. Express it! Expressing your concern in a calm way and then acting upon it allows you to relieve the stress and tension built inside of you. Assuming the blame game as a successful tool does not always work. Blaming the school or sometimes yourself, may seem appropriate, but it creates an emotional roller coaster ride. It is not always the teacher, the school, or your fault. Sometimes, it is simply a misunderstanding of information. For example, a common misconception is that you got what you wanted because you screamed and yelled at the school or teacher. You can be mad, it is okay to be hot and mad, even angry. Yes, some parents were angry at me too. But, where did it get them? Even if they did get everyone's attention, then what? What did they want? Everyone was listening and watching. The spotlight was on them. The same question is posed to you, what do you want the world to know about your situation, your child, and you?

The confidence you possess is crucial to long term healthy school relationships. This means leaving behind old mindsets of disgust and moving forward with action. Focus, instead of taking out your frustration with everyone. It may seem like you are speaking hot air that goes up like a hot air balloon and comes back down flat. All that hot air warmed the atmosphere. Now what? Do not burn bridges! It may be the same bridge that you need to cross later. I have seen this over and over. Parents blamed me and then later needed my help with their child. Finding your voice is not an easy task. Some parents continue to question whether they have been heard. Stay focused. Move boldly, invest time, and clearly express your goals. Do not just say you are tired of something and then not have plans on what to do next. Say, what you mean and mean what you say.

Fired Up!

Chaos! Total Chaos! Summer is almost over. You are waiting to hear the news. Will students return to campus or remain online for distance learning? You listen to the news broadcast, sitting with your fingers crossed, hoping, wishing, praying … "Please be open. Please be open. Please be open." Once again, many governors in several states declared schools will resume using a hybrid system, where students attend school on campus part-time and staying home part-time for online distance learning. At this point, you know you need help. Some situations in the classroom were chaotic. You probably learned that your children, along with other students, were wild, off task, and chose to be selective listeners. And you are thinking, "Well, those children in those classes could not have been worse than what I went through these past three months." This is how you have felt the past few months and still a little right now. As you spend time thinking about what bothers you, you will see the positive. "Positives?" you scream! "What?!" Yes, you will see the positive results that you have achieved even if you could not see it. You are a work in progress.

Many parents have had the experience of walking into a school and felt like they were not wanted. This is enough to get you upset. As a parent, you will get tired of constantly begging the school staff to listen to you! You will also get tired of asking your child, as well. "Listen to me. Sit up. Sit down. Be quiet. Follow directions … do this and do that." You get tired, I get it. You want educators to listen … Listen to your heart's cry. You just want to be heard. And we hear you.

There are many things that separate the good parents from the bad parents. Use your voice, as I say to my younger students. Use your voice. Use your mouth. Use your words. You may have experienced a blazing hot issue. So hot, that people around you cannot stand being around you. What do you do with all that anger?

Once you calm down and stop crying, spend time looking at the situation and then make a wise decision. Just like when we tell children to listen and follow directions in class, this is a similar moment for you. Listen to yourself and then make a change.

Finding ways to control your anger, while managing your child both at home and in the classroom is challenging. During these past few months, you may have kicked, yelled, and screamed, "COME GET THESE KIDS!" I know you mean well. You are disheartened by your circumstances. We are in a new era that is shifting every moment. Times when you do not know what to do or how to do, or even want to do anything, there is help. You are still fired up. Things could turn upside down, enough for you to run out the door, but there is help.

For example, you found yourself fussing and cussing at your child and all sudden, out it came, you said something you should not have said, or did something you should not have done. Help! Come get these kids! Rising your child is your life assignment. Yet, there are many supporters which could or does include family members, social workers, and guardians. You can receive help while raising your child if and only if you feel overwhelmed with the responsibilities.

There are many ways to deal with "hot" issues and concerns. I absolutely advocate for expressing your anger. It is an emotion that we all have. We all, teachers, social workers, psychologist, administrators, and even ministers become emotional. It is not easy getting those noticeable moments out of your system. You have feelings too. But when you are finished stewing, critical answers await you. Now is the time to take that same hot air you had earlier and voice your concerns. Take the stress and frustration you have and turn it around for something good. You are growing in your role to becoming an expert.

Here are tips on taking your concerns to another level:

Tip #1: Start a prayer or support group with other parents

Tip #2: Pray for your school, staff members, and those associated with the school

Tip #3: Host meetings with other parents to plan new changes

Tip #4: Gather books and materials that help you and your child

Tip #5: Host workshops as the keynote speaker or invite speakers

Tip #6: Find the help you need

Tip #7: Be the change

Tip #8: Focus on doing better

Venturing out to solve your problems is tough. By using the suggestions above, you have an excellent start. You have now adopted and created new ways to improve the situation. Improving the situation helps the future for your child and generations to come. Now, I know you might be thinking, "How will my input make a difference?" Well, making any move is progress. It starts with you. Gather other parents and discuss frustrations and concerns that deeply move you. Once information is gathered and processed, proceed to helping make your child's school a better place for them and all students.

Furthermore, in laying a foundation for constructing concerns that displease you, meditate and pray about it. Prayer always works. In recent years, some public schools allowed mom prayer groups, parent prayer groups, and youth prayer groups to reserve rooms for hosting prayer meetings after school and on weekends. Prayers or meditation allowed you to focus on the heated issue and your attitude while resolving issues with either teachers and administrators or your child. The freedom to pray eventually equips you for the next step in freely voicing your concerns. In subtle ways, you are bringing attention and adjustments to a system that is evident for change. Prayer sets the tone for an atmosphere of hope and aligning with what matters for students and staff. I know that all too well because I was that silent praying teacher and advocate.

Interestingly, one of the school's where I taught now holds evangelical church services in it every Sunday. They have been there for the past 10 years. Although, I had been gone from that school years before the church arrived, I learned that the school atmosphere during the week is remarkable. By starting a prayer and support group, it ensures that everyone is on the same page or at least coming together to get on the same page. Supportive parenting groups are valuable and golden. They are a powerful tool to igniting the power in you and your child along with others. In this case, parent groups build support in combating concerns before eruptions. Though difficult, it takes teachers and schools to coming together in making lasting changes. In the end, wherever you lack leadership, your child's school, more than likely, can support you.

Stay Focused

Still mad? Still expressing how tired and upset you are of the child's school or that you are now home schooling? How could your behavior change with this new norm of distance learning? Are you able to handle the pressures and minimize these behaviors? Surprisingly, you have the answer. You can help yourself and your child's school. Believe it or not, some schools do not have all the answers. They are looking for your support just as you are looking for theirs.

Maybe you are that parent with one, two, or many skills. In between those times of not working online or taking a break, find time to develop a schedule for teaching or supervising new skills for your child. For example, maybe you were a majorette, drummer, or drill master in a high school or college band. Reflecting on your skills as a marcher or drill master, teach a class or group of students on stepping drills. Along with stepping, you could include teaching songs or dancing. Or use your cooking and baking skills to make delicious food snacks that could lead to a business. Develop a cooking or snack class where you create a new meal or dish. Just make sure you invite me over to sample your new food item before it displays in the store!

To your credit, you are focusing and enjoying what you do instead of being upset about distance learning or any issues in the school system. You are stepping into a new you while being with your children. Do not be shy, channel your inner talent and dive in. You will be okay. You will be amazed at how you accomplish this task while still working at home and now teaching your child a fun skill besides academics.

What is best about being at home with your child is you create your own time for fun. Of course, if your child is online learning, you will not want to interrupt their class so schedule around it. I suggested a few skills, now it is your turn find what works for you. With these new classes showcasing you and your child's skills, hopefully they will continue to perform at 85-100% in all academics, even though the focus was on home schooling.

Some schools have several dynamics that may or may not grab the attention of children who do not desire to participate in learning a new skill such as: selective listening, not following directions, talking back, not sitting in their seat, not performing well in class or with homework assignments. So, when you are sharing your talent and skills in school, be aware of students who will not participate. Since all children do not learn the same, identify what works and begin there. The skill that you present, it is something the whole class would enjoy. What does it offer? Have you familiarized yourself with the school's expectations and rules? Do you know what off task looks like? Knowing them will be your first indication when a student is off task while teaching your skill to them. Take note on how many students follow the rules and expectations and how many do not. This way you will know how to prepare the next time and make everyone's time useful. For those who would get off task help them. You may have to make a goal chart for them, to help them be a part of the reward everyone will gain from this fun activity. The goal is to have all the students participating.

And there you have it; you are helping the teacher win. It can work. So, use your skills! You do have them. Oh, yes, you do! Become the expert and show off a little.

Unfortunately, not everyone may like what you share, but you will get a few to support you. It will be cool to come during the school day and share your expertise. They will welcome your support. Some schools will be open to you showing up and sharing your expertise. You are a team, work together. They are helping you with your needs and you are reciprocating with your help.

Show up!

What continues to motive you to keep going? What brings you joy besides your little one? What makes you move into action? Take all the energy and show up, not just show off with your attitude. Today, it is about you. Make it your day to show up at your child's school and help. Even if you show up and sit in the class, you are helping.

Now that you are this at this point in the book, this is not the time to give up. When building new working relationships with the school, take charge. Most people like to take charge and run things. You do not have to be a big show off but show that you care and be forceful about it. What I mean by taking charge, is finding out the resources and places that will help you become better and implement some of those ideas with the school and your child. We all do things differently. In your case, doing something is the key. I believe in you. Change is vital for the school, you, and your child.

Extending your hand means doing more than you have ever done. Let your child see that you can do it. Let them see you making tough decisions. We learn and grow from others. You do not have to suck up to the teacher or principal, just be you. Let them see that you are genuine and capable of handling situations, if not all of them. They will not mind that you are fresh and learning, taking baby steps following through on assignments, and taking their suggestions. They are there for you.

Distractions will come but keep going. Sometimes

your loud voice could be the distraction and interruption they need to see and hear clearly. Remember the talk earlier about being mad as fire? Yes, use that hot coal to put out the fires that disrupt your child's education or disrupt you child from attending some schools. Always look for another bright day. Sometimes those bad days, are what they are, bad days. You must know a brighter and better day is round the corner.

Being at home maybe not be so bad after all. You can always learn outdoors. Activities such as walking to the park, taking a trip to nature gardens, or biking are ways to learn too. Sometimes children just want to be seen, heard, and moveable. Whatever activity you choose, choose wisely. No one likes working with students with bad attitudes. This is when counting the days to the end of the school year becomes common. Is there a right or wrong approach to helping at school? No. The key is offering your support as much as you and getting help with what you cannot do.

You may not admit now, but you once you start taking baby steps you will find the balance of working at home while teaching your child fun and manageable activities.

It works! It works! Showing up works. When you participate, everyone wins. The key to getting over your hot fire of concerns is participating. Whether you participate at home or at school when is it fully safe to return, be proactive. When you are all done, the smoke passes, the lava settles, you look up and you see the beauty of something new. Some people say, causing the fire is deadly, but in some cases, fire refines and makes for better objects.

Do not give up! As you remain positive through the transitions, you will see your breakthrough. While making a change, you are in charge. It could be hard, but you can do it! Absolutely look for a better day. In the end, maybe the school will hire you.

Chapter Six

Radical Move

Some matters may seem trivial, but the news of another young African American man being murdered stirred everyone, enough to get everyone involved in making greater changes. The difficult scenes of murdered victims and conflict are real issues that many children witness throughout their daily lives in their neighborhoods. The reality for many children sitting in the classroom of urban schools is they live and breathe such powerful scenes that are too mature for them to understand. But this is their life. These issues can create heavy tension and smoke in the classroom and throughout the halls of the school.

Certain school settings are filled with students being off task, loud, disruptive, ignoring rules, and expectations while teaching is going on. The classroom setting could be overruled and the noise level extremely overwhelming by the students while teachers were swamped during it. Yes, teachers get hot tempered and lose their cool too, especially when children are disrespectful to all adults. This is another good reason why adults in the classroom helps.

For some teachers, the challenge of working with children is ensuring that they are well disciplined, respectable, and able to work with others. What I have seen from students is “bad” behaviors they learned either at home, family members, or from their neighborhoods. After witnessing this, I was convinced that I had my work cut out for me. And there was work cut out for parents too. Some of the same children who came to school exhibiting those behaviors, typically had their peers join in with them. However, some children really did not know or understand the behaviors they were exhibiting which included: talking back, not following directions, disrespecting themselves, and adults. By teaching them to set smaller goals for themselves, take ownership of their behavior which in turn motivates them to make better choices.[3]

Those were expectations and lessons I taught in my classroom. Lessons that I strived to implement and instill in children so that they were better able behave with everyone everywhere they went. Some children in the schools certainly needed a lesson on respecting others. They needed to start with that and continued until it became a part of their life. Many of these children loved talking back. Strangely, these children did not understand why they talked back or what they were doing.

For a moment, while working as a substitute teacher in various schools, I recognized students off task, disrespectful, rude, and not willing to learn. I also learned that was the reason many substitutes did not want to work at some schools. They absolutely refused to work or show up.

"Who is running this school?" This is what I

---

[3] Cohen

always asked at times when I witnessed the students out of control. When I encountered out of control issues at some schools, it made me wonder, who was in charge. There was a plethora of unmet needs in the building. For example, I noticed children running in and out of classrooms before class sessions began and throughout the day. I would see children eating breakfast and throwing breakfast items around the room or on the floor, while making paper airplanes and throwing them. There were students who spoke out of turn, when not spoken to. Some children became upset easily, while not listening to others or they chose to use selective listening ears. There were some students roaming the halls and making loud noises instead of being in class learning material. It seemed like not only were expectations not followed, but students seemed to behave and do whatever they wanted. At times, I could not tell who was louder, the students or the teachers from all the yelling in the halls. That scene was enough to make someone think twice about working on that campus. Sometimes I wondered if some schools enrolled all the behavioral students from every school. It seemed like most of those students had no home training skills.

Even though, some schools had expectations and rules, students seemed to ignore the rules. Who was committed to enforcing these expectations and getting students back on track? It is important to learn about classroom settings for the purpose of making radical changes. This chapter shares observations of students in schools where I either taught or advocated with families as well as give tips to parents in making radical moves.

When I was a substitute teacher, I had a teacher who left excellent lesson plans and notes for the day. I appreciated the teacher leaving well developed lesson plans. It took away the misguidance of student behaviors for that day. Those elaborate lesson plans certainly made a difference. However, sometimes those well thought out lesson plans were written so well, it was too much for me to catch up with the student's regular class routine. Those organized lessons plans showed the caring need of those teachers and that they knew their students. But, in most instances, it worked.

On another day in class, I had 18 students. Out of those 18 students, only one student performed well all day. That day, the other students were rude, disrespectful, not disciplined, out of order, unruly, talking back and argued with me. I sense they did this because they were used to doing this. Someone allowed for their behaviors to remain.

Another time, I arrived at a school, I had to wait 45 minutes before they sent me to a classroom. I ended up having to wait awhile before being assigned to a classroom. Finally, I was given assignment.

When I first walked into the classroom, I was amazed at what I saw. The classroom was a mess. Papers, pencils, books, and balled-up paper towels were everywhere. The teacher's desk was a mess – a complete mess. I was wondering, what did they teach? Are the students able to learn in here? What kind of students came to this messy class? Well, despite the atmosphere of the room, I was not there for that. I was there to make a difference for at least one child. I was there for all of them, but if I reached one, it was an accomplishment. Consequently, I was able to teach and make a difference for the students in class.

I wanted you to see the picture of what went on in schools. Thus, a magnificent reason for you to appear at school and participate. I am not saying, you must show up and everything will change for the better, but I am saying, work more with your child's school schedule. Schools really need your help. They have changed over the years. Every school has their own way of pushing and moving forward.

Unfortunately, some of the classes I subbed for had

many teachers leaving or taking more days off due to what they encountered in the room. For many of those teachers, those schools were not what they expected in a teaching career. Given, some schools did not have to deal with many chaotic and out of control behaviors. I would like to think that due to changing in the economy, some schools and teachers were given the short end when teaching professions were rising.

I noticed vast differences between elementary to high school students and staff. The list of these expectations could run long, students from both schools did not seem to understand expectations. A few of those expectations on the list included: listening to lessons, appreciating others, and remaining on task.

On many occasions, students spent their time arguing and feuding with me about what I was giving them to do that they did not get much done. At least, I was able to teach something to get their attention.

Ultimately, each school must decide what works best for them. Their focus was to constitute character in students. It very well could be, what you see is what you get. But it does not have to be that way. Being consistent and willing to change is vital to the success of the school. Here are more of my random observations of student behaviors from these classrooms.

Well, it was another day of listening and watching rude and disrespectful students. Students were off task and acted like preschoolers and I was not working at preschool. They acted like they could do whatever they wanted when they wanted with whom they wanted. There seemed to be no boundaries and discipline for any of those students. They kept getting up and walking out the class when they wanted too. Many of those students kept eating candy, chips, and drinking juice while sitting in class, even though the expectation was clearly no eating in class. They were rude, constantly out of their seats, disrespectful, and had low self-esteem.

In another classroom, once I arrived and entered the classroom, it was a mess. The whole floor looked like a tornado hit it. On this day, I was the second substitute. The first substitute sat in that room while it was looking extremely bad. When we switched, I sat for a while not cleaning the room, then I could not take it any longer. I had to have the students clean the room. I had them clean the floor and the whole room. And, they did! Thank you, Jesus!

The rest of the day went well. They listened and were attentive.

However, watching their behavior that day was another reason why I choose to teach. I wanted to make a difference in the lives of children who behaved this way. As matter of fact, the numbers of African American teachers had gone down. I have noticed that there were few of us at several schools in my city and in a few surrounding states. Aside from the teaching profession, more schools seemed to be flooded with African American behavioral support staff. Speaking of radical change, parents could help with this change of seeing more teachers of color.

At least, what I did notice was many African American children whether in elementary or high school respected me as the substitute teacher.

A fortunate opportunity was when students sat and listened attentively to my mini lectures about life, especially about several African American contributors and history in America. We talked about more contributors than just the well-known few such as: The Reverend Dr. Martin Luther King, Harriet Tubman, Fredrick Douglass, Jackie Robinson, and Nelson Mandela. Somehow those individuals always seemed to be the main and only ones displayed in classrooms or schools that I worked in. It is not just about American, or African American history, it is about their family history. Where was more culturally relevant information? For those students, it was not about where they were at that moment, but where they were going. These students will get it. Even after sharing a little Black History, there is still a lot that they must learn. There is so much for them to learn. So much.

There were times that I showed up at schools, and it was noticeable that there was absolutely no management from leadership. There just simply seemed to be no correction, discipline, or mismanagement. The teachers and educational assistants seemed to always manage the students by themselves. Other substitute teachers including myself had to overlap and work multiple jobs. That was a lot of work in some schools with a few staff members. Though it worked well in some schools, it did not work well in other schools.

Incidentally, some school personnel felt terrible that I had to see those unpleasant classrooms and rude behaviors. I was used to seeing it. I did not like it, but I had seen it enough to know what to do. This took years to manage. After all, whose fault was it anyway? Hmm, I do not want to make a fuss on this now, but I encourage parents, teachers, principals, and everyone start now and make a change for a better school environment.

During my years of subbing, I admit there were days that I did not want to teach at some schools. Absolutely, not! But there were schools that I enjoyed going to and they were not that different either, but I knew which students to with work. It seemed like choosing my battle at schools was the goal. I was thankful for all the opportunities of being in those schools. Whether it was at a high school, where the students were old enough to make their own decisions or elementary and they still needed more guidance, those years were still good teaching moments. The good news was I was able to still help and reach the students that needed the help. With the descriptions above of many classroom settings, I was able to tackle my goals and remain faithful to my assignments.

There were certainly many exceptional opportunities of subbing in several schools. On another occasion, I enjoyed my substitute teaching assignment. That day, I was able to meet students who took their education seriously. At that school, I learned that the staff worked smart to change the atmosphere, paradigm, and mindset of the students from negative mindsets to positive thinking. Those students were eager to learn. It was not just the class that I was in, but all the other classes. These students showed me that they cared and wanted to learn. That they were smart and capable of excelling. They shared a lot with me that day. That was refreshing. Refreshing because I was not pulling teeth to get anything out of them. They were willing to share and take information and achieve their goals. That day, I enjoyed being there, listening to them and teaching them new information.

Going Back to School

You are learning better ideas, suggestions, and tips on what you can do as a parent at your child's school. There is a lot to learn. Yes, in some ways it is like you are going back to school. And that is not a bad idea. Schools, children, and families have changed. We decree better change is on the way. What is important to you is important to teachers in schools and that knowledge can be passed on to your child. What are you preparing for?

Some parents wanted to let go. When I asked parents about their child, many were concerned and wanted to see their child succeed in life. One way to help with that was by attending meetings at their child's school. After each school meeting talk to those in attendance to see what they are doing. Everyone has their idea of success. Do not feel bad if your idea works or does not work, the main goal is your input. So, when an idea comes up, share it. This is how you respond to putting your concerns into action.

You may ask, what goes on during this conference nights? Conference nights are good nights to explore and observe what extra programs the school has to offer. Most times everyone from the staff to other parents and children are relaxed. It allows for open discussion and longer opportunities to share what is on your heart. I always loved these nights. It gave me the opportunity to share and lecture the importance of education.

Create a Plan

Since you are already home being creative, uncover more of those hidden talents. In the beginning, it can be hard developing a plan. Preparation is needed when you are moving to the next level. Whether it is your first time or last time, you can do it. It is all about what you do. It is about taking steps to have fun. Even though, learning how to read, write, and work math problems is essential, making quality time with your children and family members is crucial. So, step out of your comfort zone and step into that funny zone and create laughter.

Students – most of them love to compete, they love to be on teams. What ways can they compete on teams? What ways can you get them to have fun and still learn? It is about you and them creating and having fun. Students enjoy performing in front of others, especially their peers. I have been in schools, where students performing dance drill teams, singing, and playing an instrument encouraged students' higher thinking learning. You can be that rising parent starting something new and exciting at your child's school. Change the paradigm. Yes, that is you, arise to the occasion. You are important, you are the best. You are ready for this moment. This is your moment.

Ways to become a supportive and active parent:

Go to the school and volunteer your time, talents, and gifts. No matter how small or great your talent, any help is appreciated. At least, if you were in my classroom, I welcomed all help and volunteers. Some ideas for getting activities started included: cooking, art, writing, and singing classes.

You do not have to be the top chef, artist, writer, or singer to share your gift. Schools are looking for supportive parents. Another pair of eyes in the classroom, on the playground, in the gym, art, or any class at school. Teach a photography class or a class on using a game on the computer. Add some flare to what you bring. Going to school or back to school as an advocate for your child does not have to be boring. Add something and then enjoy being a part of it.

At one school, the teacher implemented "lunch power" where chosen students would eat lunch with the teacher or guest for their class. This is something that you can introduce and do daily. Students and teachers love this idea. Sometimes it is the best part of the day. Well, one of the best moments of the day.

Develop Support Groups

How can you work together? Develop parent support groups. If you are a parent and you have never participated or started a support group. Now is the time. Support groups allow you to use your voice and get heard. You will be sharing with other parents like you. These groups will empower you to make radical moves. Here are some steps on how to develop support groups

Tip #1: Create a survey inquiring about parent concerns in your school. Share with parents and administrators

Tip #2: Communicate with school staff so that they are supportive of your group

Tip #3: Create a newsletter where all parents can voice their concerns if they are not able to attend meetings

If you have never formed a group, this is your time. Make this fun. Do not allow the logistics of forming the group take out all the fun. This is an important step and move for all parents. You may be thinking it is just for you, but you are doing something to get everyone involved. If you have more steps on how you would create a group, add them to the list. Remember, you are a parent making a radical move.

I am often reminded of parents who had a tough time with their children and did not know what to do. Finding the right person, a group helps during a crisis. You must be willing and able to compromise, work with others, be willing to change, accept criticism and move forward. You want to represent your child well as the parent.

Teaching takes a lot of patience. Being a parent more patience. You may be that parent who has little to no time. But this guide will help you start in the right direction. Move to the next level as a successful parent who can do anything. You are your child's hero!

Do it! It is tempting to give your child the world

and expect nothing in return. No, you still must teach, nurture, love, comfort, help, give, and share ideas with them. That was a mouthful. I am amazed that you have reached this point. It is like a time when I did not tell the students to do something nice, but they did it anyway. I guess being nice shows. This is what you want … nice but stern.

Reaching Them

How do you teach and reach your child and prepare them for the world? Work on developing your learning plan. You do not have to be a rocket scientist or math whiz. I mean those are okay, but it takes time, your time. Reaching your child means spending time with them. It means finding out what they like or do not like. It means being there in the moment with them. Your radical move is being there and supporting them. I know you are working on that now.

Children will give you – what you teach them.

Teaching them their worth and that they loved and valued. When you teach children morals, respect, and common sense, this helps them both in the home, at school, and wherever they go. They may feel and tell you what to do or that they know it all but test them with knowledge and keep testing them. They also may tell you what they need what they need to do, and what they do not need. Children need constant direction and redirection.

You may feel like you are overloading them with information, but they will be alright, after all, they are gaining an overload of information from the internet. They do need life lessons. Do not allow your children to say that you are not teaching them anything. If no one else teaches them on life lessons or lectures to respecting themselves and others, make sure you sow that knowledge, because, if you do not, the world will confirm to them that, "right is wrong" and "wrong is right." Your little ones will think the same way too unless you intervene. Oh yes, they may argue at and with you, but in the end, they will appreciate what you are doing for them.

Here are some tips on how you can reach your child:

Tip #1: Make a list of who they are and what is important to them

Tip #2: Write down any concerns you or they have

Tip #3: Solve their concerns by asking questions

What works:

Flexibility

Being stern

Following rules or a point system and chart

Staying on task

How to keep your child on task:

Remain consistent

Talk to your children

Lighten up

Use a stern voice at times, but also a sweet loving voice when needed

Use technology such as tablets, phones, computers, etc.

In conclusion, my experiences not only helped open doors for parents, but it allowed parents see inside the classroom. But this was the reason why it was so important for me to help parents navigate the school system.

As a parent all you can do is give your best. Ups and downs come with life. Sometimes life situations are easy and sometimes they are not. Refuse to give up and make a radical move.

Chapter Seven

From Broken to Diamonds

Once upon a time, there was a young boy named, Mephibosheth. When he was six years old, his nurse was carrying him in her arms. While she was running, she fell, and one of his legs was broken.

Years later, he was invited to a King's house. The King was excited to see him because he knew Mephibosheth's family, especially his grandfather very well. As a matter of fact, this king was good friends with Mephibosheth's late grandfather. While sitting at the table, the King shared stories about Mephibosheth's grandfather. In a gesture of love, the King told him that he would restore and give back to him everything that belonged to him, even though Mephibosheth did not know what he had lost.

The King wanted to show his kindness and generosity. As the King shared with him, Mephibosheth quickly added his sorrow. He added his poor condition, as if to say, "King, do you see me. I am not worthy of what you want to give me. I am nothing." Yes, the young boy said, "I am nothing." You see, Mephibosheth was now a young man with low esteem who did not think highly of himself. He felt his condition was not worthy of being outside amongst others and certainly not in the King's palace at his table.

Well, the King listened and still insisted on giving him all that belonged to him. The King even had his servants serve this young man. The King wanted to do this for him.

In the end, Mephibosheth ended up with more than expected and he was able to sit at the King's table for the rest of his life. I shared this story to say to you my friend, the excellent parent that you are right now, look up, you are now at the King's table.

You may be that broken parent, struggling to make ends meet during this pandemic. You may have felt violated and separated from teachers and administrators during this pandemic …From those whom you could have helped you front, center, and up close. Your fractured pain has undergone its own in-house surgery. Life interrupted! Your lifestyle of working around the clock and now your child's life interrupted. Disrupted by COVID-19. You have felt cut off from school resources and conversations that propelled you to move forward. Broken! You found yourself broken from the body of school believers.

School may or may not have started, but you are still at the same place with the same thoughts of intimidation, misunderstanding and misinterpreting the school system. Added to this is the contradictions and bickering of governmental officials chartering in unclear waters of the pandemic and distance learning for children.

Whether it is the school to prison pipeline, juvenile criminal justice or governmental systems, these systems are broken. It is a reminder of the accountability of education in a broken system. All you are thinking is, you are still lost. You still do not have control over your child's education or actions. You have a computer, laptop, or iPad, but you still do not know how to ensure that your child excels from there. Your anxiety had been running high and you have been on a downward spiral. You still feel stuck.

Perhaps you have read the earlier chapters of this book and still said, "What? … What am I doing right and what I am doing wrong? … I cannot do what I see others doing … Something must be wrong with me." That same scream and fired up spirit is still in you. On top of this, you are still hurting inside because you are either laid off for a while or the long haul. You are still hurting because your child is still hungry for natural food and starving for education. You are wondering how to better help with their education. You are still wondering how to survive.

You are going through like never before. The same generational (family) situations such as poverty, lack of education and illness keep finding you and telling you to stay there. What you were taught itches to remain. You look at your past and think that is where you should be. Your feelings, body, and other issues are comfortable living in despair. Certainly, your mind is saying, "Why step out and pursue success now? Why move forward, learn, or do something new?" I say to you. "PUSH!"

Yes, life can send you heavy blows. You are going one direction and the wind from all four directions, North, South, East, and West comes in strong …blowing all your hard work and enthusiasm.

Well, like the Mephibosheth's story, someone, a queen, a king, businesswomen, businessman, doctor, lawyer, minister, or teacher is there to bring you into a new place. Like the King, there are people in the right place willing, able, and capable of doing something special for you. You do not have to continue to look down at yourself or see yourself as nothing. Shift! It is your time and season to sit at the King's table.

Receive all that you lost and all that belongs to you. No matter your family background or what heritage you come from …no matter if your family chose to stay in poverty. You and your child matter. Push out and make changes for the next generation. Make changes for your child's generation. Now you and your child will eat at the King's table. You not only will eat, but comprehend reading, writing, and math. Even when that thought comes back and you question yourself, remember you and your child are worthy and precious. You both are broken vessels becoming pure shiny diamonds.

As the 90's went by and the millennial years arrived, there were more children showing up with multiple issues. One could say, it was a crazy world in our schools. I was a teacher adding on more job titles and hats. The issues of children going from home to home, lacking sleep, living in poverty, and not having enough food was beginning to become more of an appreciative lifestyle for many children. However, I knew some families did not want to be in those positions and they needed someone in their corner to help guide them.

The more I taught, the more I encountered children who were still hungry after eating school breakfasts and having morning snacks. I encountered more children arriving to school with several concerns over home life. And no matter what time school started, I encountered students arriving to school and quickly falling asleep in class. That did not bother me because I knew why many of them were tired and sleepy. They were tired and sleepy because of either lack of rest or conflict at home with their parent(s). The new norm had become that public school children were showing up to school with more challenges – challenges that kept them from learning how to read, write, and work on math.

Was there a time when you were swamped with

several responsibilities and no matter how much you wanted to catch up and remain caught up … you found yourself behind and heartbroken? Or maybe even physically broken?

When a person is broken, they feel damaged and separated from others. The brokenness has crushed and disrupted our lives. How many times have you seen broken glass, a broken pot, or anything broken? Sometimes it may just have a small crack, or long line going through that will get bigger, or even a small chip from the item. When we see this, we tend to either throw the whole item away or get some clue and put it back together. Typically, that is what we will do. Unless you do not want it because it has a crack or chip in it. As you sit there and ponder what is best for you and this item, you discover that even if you get rid of it, the problem you solved was temporal. When we see broken glass or vessels, we tend to walk over it or see it as used and useless. We say to ourselves; no one wants this. I would not give this broken item to anyone. Who would want this broken item? The truth is we all have the choice to either get rid of that broken item or fix it and keep it. What do you choose to do with the brokenness? After all, we all become emotionally side-tracked through great life experiences.

That was a little how I saw the students that walked through the doors of my classroom and any classroom I stepped into. The many times that I had to mentally become broken to understand the families that I served. Growing up in a Christian home, I was sheltered from many things in life, so I did not experience the trauma and drama many of my students were living with. So, when it came to teaching and helping my families, I could not just overlook them, look them up and down and assume my life was better than theirs.

Throughout my teaching experiences, I have seen many children show up broken mentally, emotionally, and physically. Children with screaming tantrums when they did not get their way. Children who were able to express their feelings. And, for the children who were not able to express their feelings on what was going on with them, showed off by acting out.

I am talking about adults and children who were broken … broken to the point that they were ashamed to share what they went through. They were too afraid to let others know how they felt or who they were. Broken people do not want anyone to know their situations or see the pain in their eyes. I saw them walking around, showing up at school, but hiding inside. They hid and kept their feelings to themselves. At the same time, while broken, these same adults and children were living with masks, yet moving around. I have also watched parents going through too. If you as an adult felt that way, think about how children felt when they were faced with situations that left them alone and heart-broken? This was what many children attending school go through during the school year. With the times that we live in, children are living with violent adults more than ever. For some, the adults are their parents or someone close to them. And sadly, bad things happen to many children in their homes. Thus, becomes that way of escape for many children. Parents are not the only ones screaming, "Come get these kids!" Young people are also silently yelling, "Come get these parents." Broken situations happen in families, in communities, churches, in the business marketplace, and even in schools. Underneath, both adults and children are gems and diamonds waiting to shine forth. Ironically, they must be broken to see the shiny diamond inside.

When we are born, we do not decide on being poor, illiterate, or born into a family filled with violence. We do not ask for that, but some-how we end up there. I saw children like this my whole life.

When I was younger, I noticed my friends or

children my age where I lived were in these situations. First, I thought it was cool because they could do anything, until I learned that their parents were not nurturing or caring for them. Some of the same type of behaviors I saw in children growing up were now the same behaviors and situations that I witnessed as a teacher.

At the start of my teaching career, I made home visits. I knew that visiting families at their home was vital to understanding and getting to know them. Many of the families that I had over the years, always welcomed a visit from me. It was a way of trusting me and knowing that I understood them no matter their surroundings. This was what I enjoyed most, connecting, acknowledging, and appreciating them. Family values are important to me as teacher and educator.

As a teacher, one of the most pressing issues I saw was many children struggling between home and school life. For some children, showing up at school was their scapegoat, their secret hiding place, and their safe home away from home. Children under the age of seven typically did not understand what is going on at home, but simply misbehave.

I heard about family situations during show and tell time or sometimes unexpectedly from children. Sometimes it was difficult to tell which stories were real and were made up. As time went on, I learned more real stories outweighed the made-up stories. Sometimes children played games against the teacher and their parents. I was alarmed, yet, realized it was something children do.

Sadly, there were situations when parents did wrongful acts against their children. This is like the boiling point in chapter four, but more serious. I was not a psychologist, nurse, or doctor, but a concerned teacher where some of those situations happened. As teachers we see unfortunate and fortunate situations. Though, I found myself saying, "LORD, help me, I feel overwhelmed!"

Teaching and working with families were a great opportunity but certainly not one for everyone. I had high needs and at-risk children. Children who were rude and disrespectful. I noticed on many occasions the social setting of the school could have been the cause. What I will be sharing were real situations that happened throughout my time of teaching.

All the stories that I share have a common thread from being broken to becoming diamonds. These students and parents were gems breaking into a culture and classroom of love. They resembled caterpillars breaking forth from their cocoon ready to live and share to the world their beauty. These situations did not happen all the time, but there were a few incidents that I was either involved in or close too. I am not condoning these situations but sharing for the purposes of realizing that wrongful things can happen to children resulting in them being broken and becoming diamonds.

I began my third year as a teacher. One day after school, I received a visit from a police officer. Seeing the officer made feel uneasy. I was not sure why she was showing up. I knew I had done nothing wrong, but I was curious why I was receiving a visit. The officer told me they were there because a parent reported to them that I had hit their child. What? Hit their child! I was shocked and appalled at what I heard.

The officer went on to tell me that the parent reported that I put a mark on their child, but they did not have any more evidence. They asked me a few questions about the parent and wanted to know if I did put a mark on the child. Of course, I did not put a mark on the child, but was wondering what was going on.

Once I gave a brief statement, I was invited to the police station to make a full report. Nothing like this had ever happened to me before. That same day, I went to the police station to make the report. After hearing my report, I was cleared and free to go. The police shared with me that they felt the parent was blaming me for something they did. The parent's story did not make sense. I remember going home thinking, "What just happened?" I was accused of doing something that I did not do. Why would this parent, who I had barely met, accuse me of doing something so awful?

The next day, I called the parent who accused me of hitting their child. Unfortunately, they did not speak English well, so my questions were not helpful. I did get the social worker and translator involved to find out what was going on. I learned that the parent disciplined their child and left a mark and instead of saying they did it, they blamed it on me. They feared being reported to social services. Wow!

Once this situation was over, I learned that I had to be careful and watch what I said and what I did and how I handled children. This type of situation or any similar situation never happened to me again throughout the rest of my 28 years of teaching. It was the one and only situation. I mentioned this because some parents are responsible for wrongful actions. Teachers are mandated reporters when it comes to seeing an abusive child. It is hard identifying adults with abusive behaviors, but I never had to deal with any of these parents. Although, I did come close to it a few times.

Years later, another abusive incident was shared with me. One of my students and their sister, who was in another classroom, came to school with casts on their arms. I did not think much of the cast. However, I was going to inquire about their broken arms, but my other students had already heard a story about that student and their sibling's broken arms.

Looking at the cast and knowing my student, I knew there was more to the story. I asked the child about their arm, what they gave me was another story that did not match what the other students were saying. I had to hear the real story from their sibling's teacher. Unfortunately, their mom burned both of their right hands. The incident was immediately reported to the office and a child protection (CP) liaison and the police showed up at school to interview the students.

Later that week, we learned that they were sent to a foster home. My principal at the time met with all the staff to inform us of the situation and how to work with the students once they arrived back at school. In the following weeks, those students returned to school. They were at a foster home and ordered not to speak to the mother. Their father was not present. The foster home had custody for at least a month and a half. While these children were away from their mother, they shared how much they wanted to go back to their mom. The student in my class, constantly talked about the day they could see their mom and live with her again. Broken! Then the day came when both students were allowed back in the home with their mom. Broken system, broken hearts, or broken vessels?

Those are the dynamics and lives several children lived and breathed every day. As a teacher, I saw many children and heard some situations, but I never had to report a situation.

This is a good time, to say, there is a time and season for everything. It is necessary to note that these parents did not want to be in those positions. Some parents either left the school or received help and support from the school.

Once again, I was faced with another example of a child misbehaving in class. That time, I was at a school where there was a lack of funds, so we did not have a social worker or psychologist on staff to help solve many of the concerns our students possessed. We stepped into all the roles while being teachers. Broken systems!

Andrew had been acting out all week. He had been

seeking attention for the past two weeks. I stopped by his home one Thursday. His mom's phone number did not work anymore. I stopped by there again the next afternoon. This time, I talked to his mom on the phone. She gave me her new phone number.

I noticed something was off, because he usually was an excellent academic student and did his best to follow school and classroom rules. At first, it was as if he wanted me to write a referral for his negative behavior. Then, he asked me to write him a referral. He was itching to get out of class. He wanted to be at home with his mom. He wanted to make sure she was okay. I knew that, but I continued to press through the best way that I knew how to understand the situation, while looking to find out how much he knew.

That particularly week, he was out of sorts. He was acting strange. I knew something was going on, but what? I did not know if he was following negative behaviors from another student or his mother's boyfriend was back in the house. This is how close I worked with my families. I did not know all their family business, but enough to know and help wherever I could.

After all, while I was growing up, I was told from my parents, "what goes on in this house, stays in this house." But now there was a new generation of children, who shared everything about what was going on at home. And, sometimes they did not hold back on some information from their living space. For some reason, they unknowingly shared. After encountering Andrew's behavior, I then learned Child Protection (CP) Services made a visit to his house to access the situation. Eventually, he and his mother were cleared, and he continued doing well at school.

Allow me to tell you one more story about another student who shared the same types of behavior as Andrew. Sometimes I wondered if they were copying each other.

Lester was acting his usual self, bullying others. He really needed one on one services in the classroom. I talked to his mom about his paperwork for special education.

We were waiting administration to complete their part of the paperwork before recommending services for him. Lester really needed help with his behavior. While we were waiting, I was told to continue writing referrals on him so that we could determine later his needs. Lester had been suspended a few times due to his extreme and out of control behavior. Unfortunately, he constantly hit other students while in the classroom. He could not keep his hands to himself. He liked hitting other children. He had supervision most of the day but continued to misbehave.

The goal was to bring order and awareness to his academic and physical well-being. What I witnessed with Lester was his frustrations with order. He was a bright, young boy who was bored with programmed agendas. He learned to prompt and nag students to get their attention.

Frequent redirection and praise for when he was positive with others was an effective strategy. Broken!

An experience like this called for deeper levels of devotion to my assignment. There is no difference between teacher, student, and parent in testifying to brokenness. It is possible for all of us to feel and become broken and still get our needs addressed. With that discussion in mind, I share some benefits on working with mainstreamed students.

Here are some tips on gaining respect from everyone in the classroom:

Tip #1: Learn and get to know each other

Tip #2: Be there to listen, smile, and lend a hand

Tip #3: Help wherever needed, become observant to children who sit and or play by themselves

Tip #4: You are a parent too. Do what is best helping other children

Tip 5: Gain respect from your child, while showing respect and guiding other children

You Matter:

As parents, remaining focused on your child's concerns allowed you to determine how to work with the teacher and staff. It was important to make sure you were getting your needs met. I know, you were at work all day and you could not find the time to become active in some school meetings and activities, however, preparing now is a wise goal.

Furthermore, understanding the game of school life is acknowledging that you clearly adhere to the mission. The discussion and shared experiences on students who were broken was focused on the necessity and views of parents.

Here are a few suggestions for what to do when you feel broken:

Tip #1: Seek help from trained counselors and other

professionals

Tip #2: Spend time evaluating your circumstance

Tip #3: Write your thoughts in a journal

Tip #4: Share with family members or someone close to you about your circumstance

Pulling it all together! You matter and are important. Yet the fact remains that as a parent, you have rights, especially advocating for your child. When you advocate for your child, you are ahead of the game.

Chapter Eight

Love in Action

When it comes to educating families, love is in the equation. Of course, some school settings may look like a process of illumination. The emphasis is on immediate need for survival and creating an environment that meets social significance for families in school. Nevertheless, intimidation and distrust could be smelled miles away when parents are seeking for assurance in any school. For parents, it is about schools developing healthy relationships with them and their child along with teaching them how to accomplish established goals. As an educator it clearly is giving and gaining respect from each party to deliver passionate leaders.

After working in the school system for a few years, I returned as a parent advocate for a non-profit agency acting as the meditator between school districts in which I enrolled and advocated for families to schools of their choice. It was imperative that I continued educating families. I recognized the need and importance of students and families achieving in all schools. By this time, the number of colored students had increased to 88%-100% in charter schools.[4] The assumption of the needs of children were perceived to be greater than traditional schools.

What I enjoyed most about being an advocate was that I did not have to grade papers and bring them home with me. For the most part I felt good about my experience at the end of the day. Advocacy gave way to settling fears for parents who were bewildered with the school system. As a mediator between parents and schools, my reputation was perceived as noteworthy.

Incidentally, from the outside peering in, what appeared on display at many schools were equity specialist as a remedy for parents. Ultimately advocacy gave way into what was civil war strategies among families and

---

[4] Dorsey

schools. After all, how were these schools quickly going to fulfill the needs of parents inquiring about their child's education and change their paradox? How were these schools staking the claim of transparency in micro-culture communities? Perhaps answers were noticeably shared among administrators, yet miscommunication was still key in many schools.

After a few years of service as an advocate, the agency I worked for closed due to lack of funding. The need to continue working with families, lead me back into the classroom. Adapting to school culture surely was comfortable. That is not to say that I had glorious and wonderful teaching moments all day or all the time.

There were many experiences where I was ready to leave the school and not show up again. As much I enjoyed teaching, some schools were culturally insensitive. Upon entering the school building whether it was elementary, middle, or high school, there was a wide range of repeated defiance and unchartered waters shown by students and staff. In my point of view, there were numerous occasions of chaos in the classroom.

I realized that catering to those challenges meant recognizing the trauma in student's lives. Some children were fortunate to have teachers that often spoke polite and courteous while others were entangled with hypocritical teachers. During it all, I received wonderful comments from students and staff. Most of those positive comments came from students. I understood my calling and showed up as someone looking in from the outside and solving loopholes or areas where no one had time to evaluate. It was at this point, that I greatly appreciated my role as the teacher. However, there were benefits and pitfalls in some schools which were reminders for reevaluating safer school environments.

Based on my beliefs, I felt students were unruly towards each other and staff members. The characterization of students running through the halls at any given time and sometimes throughout the whole day revealed a lack of an undeveloped program. A sense of disrespect for other students and adults filled the air with an aroma of emptiness like a hot air balloon. Students are under the notion that this meant "whatever happens, happens" while no consequences and rules mattered. Rules were clearly not followed. Numerous unwanted conversations were stirred throughout class time interrupted valued learning time. Some students talked numerous times and did not desire to listen. I was not prepared to witness students running over adults and taking the backseat to their own education. Despite student behavior, this was a school with several young teachers perhaps under the regulation of a desensitized environment.

In addition to desensitizing environment, most of the teachers seemed like they did not care. They seemed like they were working only for a paycheck. The African

American staff seemed to be there mainly to help with the behaviors of students of color. Surprisingly, the staff appreciated that the way I managed students.

Adults seemed to care about the students. But there were no consequences for students. All I kept seeing was students doing what they wanted and refusing discipline. At least, I knew what to expect from the staff and students. Students were constantly getting out of their seats without permission to through away things, bother other students, sharpen their pencils, visit other students, and just being defiant.

They constantly talked out of turn. A few of the girls kept braiding or combing their hair in class. All of them except two of them had major attitude (talking back at adults and students). They always felt the need to make a remark on every comment and question to them.

The biggest issue was dealing with the noise in the classroom.

For example, I remember while subbing, I was scheduled to teach 4th grade, but when I arrived at school, I was switched to helping the special education students. I worked with 8th and 9th graders. All I had to do during the first two periods was sit in the resource room which was their computer room and watch a total of 5 students. Two young ladies in 8th grade gave me trouble. Well, they had attitudes and refused to do work. Sometimes when our plans change, we must be able to go with the flow.

I made it through the day. The students were quiet. They completed assignments early. They were well behaved, helpful, respectful, ready, and willing to work. They were good listeners and learners. They were exceptionally good readers. They read books all day and saw the importance of reading.

I had a good experience there. The students enjoyed and loved me. A few of them asked me to stay and come back. They were saying, we really like you. Now, this is what I enjoyed doing and how I loved to work. I can enjoy my time and space, talk, motivate, help, support, smile, do what I want, sit, and still get paid. Now that is the kind of job I enjoy. I like working when it does not feel like work.

However, I always looked forward to the days when everyone was on the same page. One of the greatest moments was walking into a classroom with a prepared lesson plan on the desk waiting for me. Noticing students coming from the bus or being dropped off, watching them get and eat their breakfast, and then starting the class with no interruptions during morning meeting. This was a lasting moment of joy that occasionally happened. When those days arrived, I had to realize that not every day was peachy.

Relatively speaking, I had to teach at schools through the good, the bad, and the ugly. Some of those days may have been viewed as insignificant and possible representing days to be savored. In fact, fun, easy, and relaxing became the norm. It made up for those unbalanced days. In other words, when students saw that their classmates were helping and everyone followed through, it was classic and bearable.

If you will want you child to grow up having a healthy lifestyle, it starts now, right here, what you do and what you say that matters. Naturally, it takes to tangle, so you will have to find the time to mingle with other parents and the school staff. Simply put, participate with your child's school activities. Do not just sit back and let teachers, other school staff, volunteers, and even students create an environment not applicable to your child's needs.

You have a voice, use it. Use your voice to express your concerns and how you feel. Use your voice and make necessary changes so that your child and other children learn well. Learning takes time. Some schools are often waiting for parents to act and organize activities, programs, sharing their expertise, or simply helping wherever needed.

Better days are here. It is not like those days when you sent your child to school and let everyone take charge and then they sent them back home letting you know how they handled it. Although some of that may still go on. Possibilities are endless, the ball is in your court. What are you going to do?

Check In

As frustrating and overwhelming it was for me, as a teacher, to encounter such powerful school settings, I know it is the same for you as a parent. How are you doing as a parent? Are you getting your needs met? Is the school listening to you? Are you being supported and not taken advantage of? As a parent, these are some questions to address while at the same time learning how to ask new questions to address your child's needs at school. Be sure to check-in with your child to see how they are doing at home, in school, and wherever you go. Getting all the detailed information that you need to make better plans. Sometimes you must check in to see how others are doing.

You are very capable to being the expert parent working with schools. The scary part is knowing what to do and how to do it well. You are not working and getting involved in your child's school to get a star on the school sidewalk, you are doing it because you care and want to make a difference at your child's school.

You are doing it to show other parents, the school, and community that yes, parents can and will get up and get out and make a difference. Some schools have potential. They know how to welcome parents and not make them feel intimidated. I often found at some schools, supportive African American staff were not taken seriously and not necessarily welcomed at the school. As if to say, they were not capable, or well off enough to find the loopholes these school possessed.

Controlled Environment

Have you ever entered a community with loud music playing on the streets, children and young adults hanging out on the streets, adults were nowhere to be found, and cars are rolling up with people smoking and drinking in them? Yes, this is the scene many children in our cities see daily. This is one reason some parents choose to transport their children across town to other schools. Now picture this; big beautiful school, grass cut, landscaped, cleans sidewalks, it looks clean on the outside, the parking lot is clean and clear, and it looks empty. You see people going in and out, but they seemed to be walking in controlled manner. But when you walk into the building, no one addresses you, you seem invisible, there are not many people who look like you, and the atmosphere does not seem enjoyable. As matter of fact, you seem lifeless walking in the building. Now which environment would you want your child to be in?

Nothing is wrong with their decisions. What I want

to discuss here is choosing the right environment and school for your child. The atmosphere for a school is crucial to your child's learning. Sure, some children and families have been able to learn in the worse environments, but if you had a choice, what would you choose? This is your time to make better choices and hold councilpersons, school board members, and representatives in your community accountable to producing better school buildings, updating technology, and closing the achievement gap to educating your child. The whole school can look relaxed. Parents remember my observations were what I experienced you will have to observe your child's classroom when you are available. Here are tips for what the classroom environment could look like:

Tip #1: Established rules posted on the wall

Tip #2: Classroom reward charts

Tip #3: Posters that are positive and bring humor

Tip #4: Students' best work displayed

Tip #5: Seating arrangements that allow all students to learn

Tip #6: Display culturally relevant material

Celebration

It is time to celebrate you and your child's accomplishments. Celebrations allow you to be free and enjoy the moment for a moment or day. Celebrations are especially enjoyable when you are witnessing success with your child. For example, when your child receives a passing score on their tests, celebrate. Or when they do well in reading, writing, and make an award-winning art project, celebrate. Reward yourself and your child whenever you both do something exciting at school, home, work, or with other activity groups. You can also make up your own moments to celebrate.

Celebrating you

Earlier, I mentioned finding time to make a

schedule so that you are freely able to take breaks. Well, this is your time and season. By this time, you learned a little of what can help you do better at school, you would have made it to the top. Even with these tips, you remain powerful in the eyes of your child. Get excited about what they are doing in school. Sure, you probably already have all those pictures and papers posted on your wall. Once you celebrate you, celebrate your child.

Celebrate your child

It is so excited to see children make strides and push themselves to learn all they can in a short amount of time. Get excited when you see them struggling to learn spelling words then all the sudden, the get it. They may start learning three, four or seven words out of 10 on a spelling test. Then, they eventually learn all 10 and master their spelling words. They are getting it. That is a huge jump and success for them. Get excited when they have made small strides in learning sight words. Recognizing your child's growth is amazing.

Promote your child

A parent showed up to school with a huge birthday cake for their child's birthday. Sometimes these were the only days that I saw parents come to the school. I know you are happy about only showing up for birthdays, but also show up unexpectedly. Surprise your child with your love.

Here are ways to promote you in helping your child:

Become their cheerleader

Assist your child with classwork, artwork, and creative ideas

Advocate for your child

Assist the school in developing strategies to help your child become successful

Talk to other families, churches, and other community leaders

Work closely with the school

Interact with other families, the teacher, and principal

Attend community meetings, gatherings, and events

Work independently or with work with others

Get involved with small community organizations

Bring the family together and share success stories

Of course, working with your child's school means showing up as much as you can. You are the driver of your child's to successes. And while out there, do not allow distractions to get the best of you or get you off course. There are ways that you can advocate for your child and become successful in the process. It takes work, determination, and motivation to achieve the goal you set forth. Before ending this chapter, I wanted to leave few pointers and thoughts on hope, life's reality, and seizing the moment.

Hope

Hope is when you know there is a solution. There

is hope for the hopeless as we so often hear during times of despair. I look back at my own experiences. I remember when my mom was dying, I was in denial, yet having faith to believe that she would pull through. Sadly, she passed after four months of fighting cancer. That was a difficult stage for me. You may have never experienced that situation or maybe you have, but it can be intimidating when your hope is shattered. You are not alone. There are many people and organizations around to help you. What advice would you give your child? How would you motivate them? What makes you the expert? What is real? The first thing in that type of conversation of talk would be to be honest and real. People are looking for help and some want help now.

Facing Reality

I often think that we spend more time looking at what we do not have instead of appreciating what we do have. I think about those who are going through a process.

To me, it is called facing reality. There seems to be something inside of our minds that refuses to allow us to bring those real thoughts to the forefront. When the thought of something I could not handle came about, what was I to do? I would run. But that was not always the answer. I learned when I was fearful, to just do it. However, over these past few years, I have matured. You may find that you matured. I have found that when I face the reality, I feel better about myself and the situation. So, I know this sounds sad, but how can you motivate, encourage, and help others feel comfortable about facing this fear when you are experiencing fear as well? The first thing is letting people know that they must be honest with themselves. This means being honest about their feelings.

You can do this. It seems hard, but when you share what is in and on your heart, you will find freedom. You are working towards improving you and your child's lives. Do your best to share with family, friends, or associates during the happy and unhappy times.

Seize the moment.

What will you do today? There have been so many accomplishments that it is difficult to learn everything in one day, one month, and even one year. What will you do today? Searching for that perfect moment? Start here and now. What is the main message you are speaking into your child's on life? How do you help them go forward? Break …Go … Set free … Rise! Parents need that boost. When you felt stuck and desperately want to get out …Rise!

I am reminded of the Book of John when Jesus healed the young man and after healing him, he told him to rise, take up his bed and walk. I say to you, rise, take what you have and keep moving forward. This is for you, the parent who has been down and out and literally feeling like there is no hope. When do you need to rise? Now. Launch out! Go deeper! Go where the other parents have not gone. It is time to rise. It is time to do what you have been hearing. There are those standing, sitting, wishing, and waiting for someone to come to them. Now that you have been empowered, soar. Walk. Run. Do not let life get you down. Think about those moments when you are sitting with absolutely nothing to say. What do you do? Start writing and celebrate.

And so, I end with what I started with, the term hope. Hope is the bottom line. Parents who feel stuck are looking for hope. You are that lifeline for your child and another parent who needs to be uplifted and empowered. You have a right to go out, share, and encourage the next parent. Stick with what you know while working on the new you. Continue to learn all that you can.

Some more tips for you:

Tip #1: Show your child what is important and how-to check-in with you

Tip #2: Allow your child time to improve in education during the summer

Tip #3: You are held accountable for your child's education

Tip #4: The library is your friend

Tip #5: Always find tutors and get help

Tip #6: Teach your child that all aspects of sports and entertainment are not bad.

Tip #7: Set priorities

Tip #8: Rest.

Tip #9: Reward yourself and your child.

Chapter Nine

Good, Better, Your Best

Before the Coronavirus pandemic, you probably would have done things differently. Now that we have come this far, do not go back to your old way of thinking. We are at a new place. You are at a new place. You probably were not even thinking about being stuck in the house for a long period of time, gaining control, and jumping over hurdles. Looks can be deceiving. When you looked out and saw what others were doing, you felt like you were not equipped to be that smart, cool parent, then suddenly you realized, you are that cool parent. It does not matter how smart you. What matters is that you are willing to do what you can to help your child grow. Only you determine how well your child grows and how well you do in this season. Do not miss your time. You can do it!

Since school was officially out what have you done with your children? Hopefully, you remained safe and found something to work on. Currently, decisions are being made whether to open school buildings or remain closed. Whichever decision comes forth, prepare for an exciting year with your child.

Consequently, what parents must understand is teachers have 20 to 25 children in the classroom and it is not easy managing all those individual brain cells. No matter how many times we saw children acting out, we had to endure teaching lessons throughout the day. What happens when the parent gets distracted? Do they excuse the distraction or get help? Throughout this book, I continued to share my experiences. Hope they have helped you.

I remember one time a parent sent me a letter explaining that I gave their child hard words. Hard words? I was not sure what that meant. I was giving appropriate words for a child the student's age. As a matter of fact, as a teacher who knew her students and families, I would only challenge the students I knew were ready. Even if they were not ready, but I knew they would do well, I talked to them and the parent allow me to proceed with words. Anyway, this parent was concerned and yelled at me. When I explained to them what was going on, they were okay with it, but still seemed unhappy. It is not wise to yell at a teacher, especially if they are helping your children grow and advance. The teacher truly does not mean harm.

Another year, I had more parents sharing with me that they felt their child should be in special education. This is okay as long you honestly believe and feel that way. If it was recommended, then work on getting a second opinion. This same year, I remember challenging this young boy in reading and spelling. He did not seem ready right away, but my educational assistant and I encouraged him to learn more. He was up for the challenge. He took the challenge and did well. This is what you want your child to do.... challenge themselves! In the beginning, I thought he was ready to spell 20 words, but he was not. He could not even say them. It was sad to see this because he was in the 2nd grade and the words were for first graders.

What happens when your child is one age, but they continue to act younger than that age? What do you do? Does it matter? When was the last time that you walked into your child's classroom to see what they are learning? These are all especially important questions. Questions like these make a difference when it comes to advocating for your child in school. This is what many parents are faced with daily.

In looking back, I appreciated all the parents I was able to help. They deserve to be appreciated. I take this time to say thank you.

Another celebration happened when I received a call from a parent who needed some encouragement and someone to help walk alongside them as their child was going through. Her daughter was a bright 7th grade young lady. She liked school but needed some help to stay on track. I helped her daughter get on track by presenting a weekly and end of the year goal chart. The weekly charts helped, and she was able to make her goal at the end of the year.

How many times have you heard these words? "Parents just don't know what to do. … Will they get it together?" Whether you have heard them or not, I have heard them. There were some parents who just did not care. You are not that parent. You are a mover and a shaker. This is about you. That parent willing and able to get what they need to succeed. Above all, this eventually is about where you and your child are going.

This is your time to shine. It is your time to become the best parent that you can be. I always shared with my students to go from being good, to becoming better, to being their best. And that is what I say to you too as the parent. Better is here. You have reached this point and now all you can do is continue to keep going forward. It is a great moment seeing parents take charge of their child's education, taking care of themselves, and taking care of business. Your business. You have come too far to let everything that you worked for slip and slide and get away from you. Better is here. Your better is here. This is the time that your hopes and dreams come together.

I know this is all about what you can do when you are stuck and believe me you are finding your way out or you are already out of being stuck. School may never be the same, but now you know what to do and how to make life better for you and your child.

Speak Up!

Speak up and let your voice be heard. Children certainly speak up. Listen to what they say because children tell the truth. They are always sharing their "real" life stories. They speak up about what bothers you and them the most. Most of you want to do something. And you shall. However, once you speak out, be ready to follow through with making changes.

But somehow you still may not want to get involved and some schools will not make you get involved. Let us not overlook that some school districts have a desire to exclude parents from getting involved. Yet, that is not the case for many school districts.

When it comes to speaking up, hold staff accountable. Some staff members are not interested in helping some children. They spend more time away from school then being there.

I remember working with many staff who spent more time being absent than present. Really! Really! I mean really! Come on now. There were days when all 19 to 25 of my students were accounted for and in class, along with me and other staff.

Children can quickly change. Sometimes children feel unhappy and left out. This is when giving encouragement helps. The reality is they are looking for your attention. They want to be affirmed and confirmed of who they are and how important they are to you. Say and show them how much you care and love them. Children need to hear this often first from you their parents and then get praise and approval from teachers. Everyone wants to hear how well they are doing. Although there are times when you must look within and become your own cheerleader. It is not every day that praise and appreciation come.

You are happy now

Wow! I hope you look forward to enrolling your child into school or homeschool and make things easier for them. You are making grown-up decisions and all the sudden, you sign your child up and enrolled them into school or settled for homeschool. All the sudden that grown-up decision becomes crazy hard to manage, too much to handle, and you are pulling your weave off and hair out. What do you do? You look up, take a breath, and tell yourself you can do it. This really is your happy moment, knowing that you can do it by yourself. And you do it, enrolled your child, learned to homeschool, and settled as their advocate and cheerleader.

Enjoy advocating for your child:

When it comes to advocating for your child, you are the one making the difference. You can watch others and model after them, but eventually it is what you do. Your child is watching you. All you need is confidence and encouragement.

Here are some suggestions for advocating for your child:

Tip #1: Get excited about taking charge and show up at the school

Tip #2: Become determined to make the changes needed

Tip #3: Develop a plan and see it through

Management at home and at school:

Having home and classroom management is key for success. Managing time in school is a lot like how you are managing your family time at home. Certainly, there are two different things going on, but if you manage your home, you can do the same with your children at school or wherever they go, for life. Children do not have full control. Find the time to teach them your expectations at home. This starts early on when your child is between the ages of two and four. They are like sponges and will soak up everything. They will remember what you teach them. Teach them well. What you are constantly passionate about let that show. Your excitement will be their excitement. Like eggs, handle them with care. They also need to know how to handle themselves without you.

Suggestions for sharing life lessons with your child:

Tip #1: Teach them what you want them to learn to have a successful life.

Tip #2: Teach them what is expected in and outside

of the home

Tip #3: Teach them they are beautiful, skillful, and helpful.

Tip #4: Say it, model it, and repeat it.

Suggestions for managing time at home:

Tip #1: Teach them right from wrong

Tip #2: Teach them what is expected when they meet new people

Tip #3: Teach them about showing up on time

Going above and beyond:

Up and above means, you are the cream of the crop. It is important to know that for yourself and for your child to know that too. We have advanced technology that makes it easier for you to be a winner – a winning parent. Take this time during the shut-down to regroup, align yourself on a new path and go for it. Of course, you will always continue to learn.

You are wanted. When it comes to gathering ideas

and making plans for a better school, you are wanted in helping with those changes. There are parents who look forward to no school. So that they can teach their child what matters to them. However, everyone is not like this. By going above and beyond, you are being supportive and accountable, helping, seeing, and making new decisions. Earlier, we discussed developing those working relationships. This helps to get to know the principal because then you can help them understand you and your family. It also helps because then you know what they believe in and how important you are to them. You can help them make better decisions about the school and future outcomes of the school

Here are ways that you can go above and beyond:

Tip #1: Be on time at events

Tip #2: Teach your child to help their peers during the good and bad times

Tip #3: Show up and help unexpectedly, without

being asked

Tip #4: Listen to the needs of the school and staff, then help them

Tip #5: Empower other parents and lead them to the front of the line

Now you have learned new ways on how to move forward in improving your ways to surviving this pandemic while staying and working at home with your child. One key to remember is remaining on task. Focusing on the necessary changes requires time and effort – time you now have or schedule to have. Get involved, strive for better, and realize you are that winning ticket.

Chapter Ten

You Can Do It!

I listened to Mrs. Finley as she shared with me her concern regarding her daughter. Her daughter, a sophomore in high school was partially blind. Mrs. Finley credited the school by announcing how well they were accommodating some of her daughter's needs. However, she was disturbed about a vital part of her of child's education. Though her daughter was partially blind, her classwork was not designed to accommodate her disability. Mrs. Finley expected that her daughter's classwork be written in braille so that she was able to learn. Since that was not in place, a frustrated Mrs. Finley approached the school. After all, her greatest need was not being met. Along with those educational concerns, Mrs. Finley also felt that she and her daughter were not treated fairly by the school staff. Once I learned that information, I helped Mrs. Finley discuss her concerns with the administrator and teachers who worked with her daughter. What I witnessed was a parent using her new knowledge to advocate for herself and her child.

A similar situation happened with another parent regarding her son. She was concerned that her son was not comprehending and excelling in his schoolwork. She was told that her son seemed bored in class. Instead of rushing to solve the matter, this parent decided to show up at the school unannounced to see what her son was not capable of doing. To her surprise, her son's seating assignment was in the back of the room. This made it difficult for him to learn material since he sat in the backrow. Upon learning this, she communicated her concern with her son's teacher and saw results days later. Mrs. Jones wanted to make sure her son received all he needed to be successful.

I attended a meeting with Ms. Sims. This was our fourth meeting. She wanted to discuss her son's academic behavior in the classroom. Apparently, he was not receiving adequate assistance from his teacher. During this meeting, the parent had to decide whether her son was going to remain in the teacher's class or move to another class. Other decisions include the following: what type of teacher is dedicated to your child's education and how will they create an environment that grasps your child's attention? In this situation, the parent removed her child and placed them in another class. It was difficult and overwhelming for that parent, but they successfully accomplished their goals. Some parents give up during that process because they feel inadequate. Most families have no idea what advocating for their children entails or how much effort it takes.

What happens when parents do not receive the help they need? Sometimes they become disheartened and leave the school with unresolved issues.

In some cases, it was difficult for parents to share their concerns. Therefore, there was a need for working relationships with teachers and administrators. They may be preoccupied, but eventually they will be ready to serve you. On the other hand, this is when advocates are helpful.

One of the greatest moments you have as a parent is representing your child well in any school district. You provide an opportunity that serves best. Remember, you can help your child. You are the adult. Know what your child is doing all the time or at least most of the time. Of course, your child will think you are strict, they all do. But setting expectations and standards will help them.

As countless school districts in all 50 states scramble to make the best decision to reopen school campuses and or remain online through distance learning, I know numerous parents still need someone to listen to and help them through this new phase of education. Many parents simply do not know how to get involved. They want to help but are not sure how to get help.

Power Up!

As a parent, you may feel powerless right now. Some of you are working full time while staying at home working with your children in school. It is home schooling and full-time work all rolled into one. While it may seem exciting, staying at home and going to school online is difficult for some parents, even parents who have been homeschooling for years are expressing burnout.

Homeschooling gives parents the opportunity to closely monitor their child's learning. Many parents have been successful with this school choice. Now many parents have quickly been thrust into the same situation of homeschooling.

Every so often, I hear parents say they cannot teach or work with their child at home. But you can! Your goal is to become aware of the options you have while at home and identify what is pertinent for your child. Use the power within you!

While you are still weighing the options, reflect on your involvement. This is the time to up your game! Sit down with your child and create goals together. Being a parent is demanding, but you must remain the parent and not your child's buddy. Whether you are the parent, grandparent, or guardian, helping your child matters. Sometimes you may need a role model, especially if you do not know what to do at school. Getting involved takes effort.

Helping your children learn can be difficult, but there are many ways to contribute to your child's academic success. Their education is important so supporting them academically, socially, and mentally is essential and viable to them. In turn, their journey of education is valuable.

For many of you encountering this new venture, staying at home to teach your child is challenging. It is a situation that calls for enthusiastic assistance. Once you have accepted the challenge, look at the task at hand, and let the work begin.

Go, Parents!

Sometimes you must be your own boss and cheerleader. You must get up and do what is right for your child. You must be the one to go visit the school, take charge, and go forth! It is encouraging to know that once you make one step, keep going.

You can do it! You will sometimes not get that pat on the back you want from others. There will be days you must do it for yourself. You must remember that all your efforts are for you and your children.

Do not allow what you do not know to do to keep you from moving forward. Everyone fails at something the first time, but it is your ability to get back up that defines you. So, get up and keep going, even when no one is cheering you on. It will take a minute, but you are able to flow. You will feel amazing when you achieve something for the good of your family. Noteworthy conversations start with knowing what you want, pursuing, and accomplishing it.

You can handle any situation that your child goes through in school or at home. You can conquer it once you put your mind to it, write it down, and do it. Open your heart and see what happens! Often, we focus on the negative and allow it to pull us down. Take the negative words or criticism, or situation, and turn it around. Look at that! You are a proud parent.

Advocate:

You are probably thinking, "What now, what do I do? How do I get involved?" This is your time to get up, get out there and support your child. More importantly is that you are now ready to excel and show your child how active you are in their school life. Advocating involves being a mediator between you, your child, and the school. When you advocate for your child, you are making decisions that are best for them. Participate, it does a body good. Just try it! Get up and find the time to get in the game. Become your child's biggest cheerleader. You and your child are a team. If you can see it, you are able to do it. Way to go! You are getting it. Count me in. We can do it, together. This is your time to show all what you can do for your child at their school.

You are somebody. It takes a lot of effort and courage to get up and start a journey you are unfamiliar with. It takes a lot, run, and go forth. Even when you do not know what you are doing, stay the course anyway. You never know where you will end up. You were chosen for this assignment, the job – the parent. You are a success. Encourage and believe in yourself.

Here are some tips on how to advocate:

Tip #1: Show up with a positive attitude

Tip #2: Know what you want for your child and pursue it

Tip #3: Collect data for helping your child learn

Research information in books or on the internet to help your child learn new material for learning subjects

Tip #4: Set your eye on the winning the game, and if you lose, keep at it

Tip #5: Schedule and manage your time

Ready for success:

Yes! You are ready for success. Preparing for success takes planning and creating goals. Exercise your brain with new ideas. Motivate, motivate, motive - remain motivated throughout the process. Once you begin, negative ideas and thoughts will enter your mind. Therefore, it is important to know why you started the process.

Shift! Make a change:

You are stuck in the home, you know a little of what to do, but you are still wishing someone would "come get these kids!" Stop, take a deep breath, look around you, and then act. It is time to make that change. Shift! This means grow and go where you have never gone before. Take on new challenges and adventures. Get ready for you and your child learning new things daily.

Become a Champion

You won! You helped your child remain successful at their child's school or in homeschool. Now that you are involved, it is time to stay involved. Aside from learning what to do and then putting things in motion, it is time to realize that you can do more. You are a champion!

Once this school year begins, put your plan into action. Start by making clear goals, aiming high, and remain persistent. You are a champion! You have jumped into a new zone. You are ready to tackle and take on the challenges with your child. You are ready to do something that makes a difference in their lives as well as at their school or in homeschool. You are a champion!

You Are A Forerunner

You are on the front line, a forerunner. One who will take it to the top and show your child that you are a winner by pressing through to the finish line. You made it! Do not allow the negative thoughts to stop you now. You proved to yourself and your child that you are in the game to win. You own this game! As you keep pressing towards your dream, you will see this happen. That time is now to see your dreams come true. Whatever you thought you could not do, you proved that you can. You took one step, a leap of faith, and accomplished your goal. The goal of advocating, participating, and getting involved with your child's school.

You are an A+ Parent

A is more than just for apples given to the teacher. A is for you, the A+ parent. A is for you the accomplished, aggressive, and active parent. This applause is for you for hanging in there and sticking with your child as they continue pursuing education. A is for staying attentive throughout your child's journey during times when you felt like giving up. And "A" is for allowing yourself to do this because you are that parent. It takes a lot to keep on track and ensure the plans of success remain with your child. You Rock!

Your children see you as a beautiful queen and king. You Rock! You are that beautiful person that held on, even when being stuck in the house only seemed like the end. You are the parent rising above circumstances discovering new joy in propelling you to the top.

Words of Praise for You:

You can do it!

Freedom lives in you!

Super parent!

You are winner!

You are a confident!

You are focused!

You are your child's superhero!

You are the best parent your child has

You Made It!

You Rock!

Again, you made it! You made it through this season of uncertainty. And you will make it throughout the rest of the year. It is time to look back at your accomplishments and move forward.

Start Your Engine

The stage is set, you are on. Everyone, including your children are watching you. What will you do with this new phase or new "normal" in education? What will you do at home and when campuses reopen?

You are like a fine, luxury vehicle. You are shiny on the outside with clean fresh oil, transmission fluid, power steering fluid, a new battery, great front end and rear brakes and that fresh new car smell. You are at the starting line. Look out into the stands and see everyone ready to cheer you on. Your biggest fan, your child, is waiting for you to take off. You receive the que to start your engine. You rev up. You are ready to go. Everything is in place and you are excited about where you are as a parent. Now you know what to do, how to advocate and stand with your child. This knowledge empowers you to make your move, to drive on this journey. It is time to move on, execute, and put forth this new revelation. You are the vehicle, so start your engine. Rev up and take off!

Conclusion

This year, 2020 started with many statements such as, "2020 vision … clear vision … or we see clearly. These were messages of hope for some people. Then, abruptly the Coronavirus pandemic (COVID-19) plagued our country, followed by the upheaval of racism, which led people to question those 2020 phrases that were chanted at the beginning of the year.

The drama of education intensified when numerous parents became stressed, frustrated, and angry when schools across America were closed due to COVID-19. The reality of home schooling, while working at home was terrifying for parents. As preparations went forth for educating children at home, many parents sought help, while others simply gave up on what they saw as an impossible task. While schools were developing strategies to ease the pain for parents working and staying home, parents were still unsure of their new "norm."

Unfortunately, articulating this new information was still not understandable for parents. Once parents realized the stay at home order would be longer than anticipated, many isolated themselves.

During it all, schools continued to connect with families to ensure the best possible solutions were being developed to continue educating students. Despite their efforts, some parents were discouraged and less empowered. The message of hope seemed miles away. Parents who believed, now were bewildered by the educational school system.

Despite what has happened this year, I still say 2020 is a year of vision … A year of clarity in education for many parents willing to sharpen their vision and see through the pandemic and the plague of systemic racism. This is a time to refocus and realign to what God designed for you, your child, and ultimately schools and education. This is the time to schedule, plan, and develop better

communication skills with your child and their school …
while at the same time, learning to have fun teaching and
working at home.

Yes, 2020 is still the year for new excitement,
challenges, and visions. The year for you, the parent, to get
up and become a better parent by participating and
supporting your children in the school building or
homeschool. Get used to the routine of being involved.
Better days are here.

Appendix A Family Schedule 1

8:00 a.m. – Family meeting

9:00 a.m. – Breakfast

10:00 a.m.–House chores

11:00 a.m.–Free time

12:00 p.m.- Lunch

12:30 p.m.–Story and nap time

1:00 p.m. – Parents time

3:00 p.m. – Snack time

4:00 p.m. – Family time/outdoors/activities

5:00 p.m. – Dinner time

6:00 p.m. – Family entertaining time

8:00 p.m. – Closure

9:00 p.m. – Bedtime

Appendix B Family Schedule 2

(Permission to print only this page – includes whole schedule)

	Father/Dad:	Mother/Mom:	Child's name:	Child's name:
8:00 - 9:00				
9:00 - 10:00				
10:00 11:00				
11:00 12:00				
12:00 -1:00				
1:00– 1:30				
2:00 - 3:00				
3:00 - 3:30				
4:00 - 4:30				
5:00 - 5:30				
6:00 - 6:30				

Father/Dad Schedule:
8:00-9:00
9:00-10:00
11:00-12:00
12:00-12:30
12:30-1:00

Mother/Mom Schedule:
8:00-9:00
9:00-10:00
11:00-12:00
12:00-12:30
12:30-1:00

Family Time:
8:00-9:00
9:00-10:00
10:00-11:00
11:00-12:00
12:00-12:30
1:00 - 1:30
1:30- 2:00

Child's Schedule:
7:30-8:00
8:00-9:00
9:30-10:00
10:00-11:00
11:00-12:30
12:30-1:00
1:00-1:30
1:30-2:00

Appendix C School Academic Check List

(Permission to print only this page)

Date ________ ________ Name ________ ________	On Time & On Task	Homework and Missing Classwork	Questions, concerns, positive or negative news, or time-outs	Teacher- Parents Signature
Reading Language Arts	Yes ________ No ________	Y / N If yes, what? ________ ________ ________ ________		
Math Science	Yes ________ No ________	Y / N If yes, what? ________ ________ ________ ________		
Spelling Writing	Yes ________ No ________	Y / N If yes, what? ________ ________ ________ ________		

Appendix D Family Decrees/Affirmations

(Permission to print only this page -includes entire affirmation)

I put God first in everything I do.

I pray and seek God daily.

I obey and listen to my parents (guardians)

I am a queen.

I am a king.

I am beautiful, healthy, strong, and wonderfully made by God.

I am an excellent student.

I am above and not beneath.

I am a link and jewel to my school, home, church, and community.

I am a part of the solution.

I am determined, dedicated, and patient.

I will take the time to listen to wise advice.

I will take the time to rest, relax, and meditate.

I will achieve my goals and live my dreams.

I will become the best at everything positive that I do.

I will treat others with respect.

I will treat myself with respect.

I will enjoy learning about my surroundings.

I will learn to sit and listen to adults who teach me.

References

Baer, J., Kutner, M., and Sabatini, J. (2009). Basic Reading Skills and the Literacy of America's Least Literate Adults: Results from the 2003 National Assessment of Adult Literacy (NAAL) Supplemental Studies (NCES 2009-481). *National Center for Education Statistics, Institute of Education Sciences*, U.S. Department of Education. Washington, DC.

Cohen, M. (1986). Intrinsic Motivation in the Special Education Classroom. *Journal of Learning Disabilities,* 19(5)

Dorsey, D. (2013). Segregation 2.0: The new generation of school segregation in the 21st Century. *Education and Urban Society, 45*(5) 533-547.

Ladson-Billings, G. J. (2000). Fighting for our lives, preparing teachers to teach African American students. *Journal of teacher education*, *51*(3), 206-214.

About the Author

Dr. Josiah Jackson, author, speaker, teacher, and actress. Josiah began her career as an elementary teacher in Minneapolis, Minnesota. As a dynamic speaker, she spoke in several high schools in Minnesota, Wisconsin, and Illinois.

She is the author of several books, including, Come Get These Kids – A Parent's Guide to Navigating the School System, the Leap of Faith Journal and God Called Her Josiah, An Autobiography by Josiah Jackson. Look for God Called Her Josiah 2nd Edition, Fall 2020.

Learn more about Dr. Josiah Jackson
at www.josiahjackson.com

Additional Books by Dr. Josiah Jackson

Learn more about Dr. Josiah Jackson at:

www.josiahjackson.com,
www.amazon.com/author/josiahjackson

Made in the USA
Monee, IL
09 October 2020